Anacrostica Dedicatoria./

H aving noe wealth to shew my gratitude
E xcept this of my Braine, how'ever crude;
N or willing to be held ingratefull where
R eceiu'd ingagements doe commaund me beare
Y ou much respect, I held it not amisse

C loth'd as it is (Sir) to present you this:
O nly my hope is (though vnlearn'd, vndress'd)
L oue will soe shadow o'r what's weake express'd
M y zeale shall not be slighted, but will find
A courteous censure, soe (Sir) shall you bind
N ature, as name to honour your brave mind./

                              Philo-poëticus./

DIVINE MED:

"Anacrostica Dedicatoria IV"
Rawlinson poetical manuscript 204
The Bodleian Library

The Elizabethan Club Series 6

Henry Colman

DIVINE MEDITATIONS (1640)

Edited with Introduction
and Commentary
by
Karen E. Steanson

Published for the Elizabethan Club
New Haven and London   Yale University Press
1979

Published with assistance from the
foundation established in memory of
Oliver Baty Cunningham of the
Class of 1917, Yale College.

Designed by Sally Harris
and set in Monophoto Bembo type by
Asco Trade Typesetting Ltd., Hong Kong.
Printed in the United States of America by
The Alpine Press Inc., South Braintree, Mass.

Published in Great Britain, Europe, Africa, and
Asia (except Japan) by Yale University Press,
Ltd., London. Distributed in Australia and
New Zealand by Book & Film Services, Artarmon,
N.S.W., Australia; and in Japan by Harper & Row,
Publishers, Tokyo Office.

Library of Congress Cataloging in Publication Data

Colman, Henry.
    Divine meditations.

    (The Elizabethan Club series; 6)
    "Published for the Elizabethan Club."
    Bibliography: p.
    Includes indexes.
    1. Christian poetry, English. I. Steanson, Karen E.
II. Title. III. Series.
PR3359.C27D5 1979   821'.4   78-25908
ISBN 0-300-02305-7

For My Son
Andrew

Contents

Preface

In the twelve years since I first saw the manuscript of *Divine Meditations* by Henry Colman, I have learned much about religion, poetry, self-reliance, dependence, hard work, and serendipity. Colman himself—whoever he was—has been alternately friend, son, brother, and enigma. I relinquish him to the literary world with glad relief to share with other scholars the mysteries I have been unable to solve and with gratitude to those who have helped me in my work.

First, many libraries have given me access to their resources. I am especially grateful to the staffs of the Sterling Memorial Library and the Beinecke Rare Book and Manuscript Library at Yale University for their thoughtfulness and efficiency. On my occasional visits, the staffs of the Houghton Library at Harvard, the Folger Shakespeare Library, the Library of the British Museum, and the Bodleian Library have facilitated my work by generous helpfulness. During my research in England in 1972, David Michelmore (Archivist) directed me through the seemingly infinite resources of the Yorkshire Archaeological Society in Leeds, and Mrs. N. K. M. Gurney (Archivist) permitted me the use of materials at the Borthwick Institute of Historical Research in York. I am also indebted to the vicars who opened their parish records to me and to two sisters, Dorothy Auty of Thornhill and Barbara Nuttall of Leeds, who relieved the lonely frustration of my quest by their knowledgeable interest and hospitality.

Next, I remember with deep respect and affection the community of scholars that has informed my studies with good advice and good example. Throughout the years, Louis L. Martz, as teacher and as supervisor of my dissertation on *Divine Meditations*, has lighted my way with his pure joy in poetry itself. I am immensely grateful to the late James M. Osborn for entrusting his manuscript to me and for sharing both his knowledge and his enthusiasm for research on unpublished materials. In 1967, John Gladson Gardner opened my eyes to the full challenge of elucidating this text. More recently, J. Max Patrick, through his careful critical comments, raised many points that I had neglected through my long familiarity with the text. The Reverend Dr. Charles L. Winters, Professor of Dogmatic Theology at the University of the South, read the manuscript and assured me that I had committed no doctrinal errors.

Finally, I thank Lois Logan and Francine Solomon, who typed the manuscript with care and intelligence.

K. E. S.

Cincinnati, Ohio

Introduction

THE TEXT

The text of Henry Colman's *Divine Meditations* exists in two manuscripts, both in the same hand, presumably the author's own since the corrections are also in this hand. The earlier and shorter manuscript (*M*), dated 20 May 1640, is dedicated to William Rokeby, Esq., whom Colman calls "my honour'd Kinsman, and most approved freind"; the later manuscript (*J*), dated 2 July 1640, is dedicated to Sir William Savile, Bart., a well-known, fiery young royalist with whom Colman can claim no personal acquaintance. I have chosen the July manuscript as the basis for this edition of the text because it is superior in most readings and because it contains nine more poems. There are twenty-five substantive changes from the May manuscript to the July manuscript, and these changes either make the meaning more precise or they correct careless repetition of a word. Although I think the July manuscript textually superior, I have included the dedicatory letter and poems of the May manuscript because of the information they provide about Colman's relationship with William Rokeby, a more significant bond than the one with Savile.

The May manuscript is a small quarto volume in the Bodleian Library; it contains forty leaves of poetry, numbered in arabic, with the title page, dedicatory epistle, and dedicatory poems on preliminary leaves numbered "ii" to "v." Its pages are 16.5 cm. high and 13.5 cm. wide and are bound in gatherings of four. It is bound in vellum on boards with gold fillet and ornaments and was formerly tied with blue strings. The manuscript, Rawlinson poetical manuscript 204, is part of the extensive bequest of Richard Rawlinson to the Bodleian Libary in 1755. Rawlinson's collection of books and manuscripts comprised nearly forty private libraries, purchased between 1714 and 1755,[1] as well as many other less extensive acquisitions. Since Rawlinson did not preserve records of the details of all his purchases, where he acquired the May manuscript of Colman's *Divine Meditations* is difficult, if not impossible, to trace.

The July manuscript is from the James Marshall and Marie-Louise

---

1. W. D. Macray, *Annals of the Bodleian Library*, 2d ed. (Oxford, 1890), pp. 249–51. Macray lists the principal libraries from which Rawlinson's manuscripts were collected and the dates, if known, when these libraries were dispersed.

Osborn Memorial Collection at the Beinecke Rare Book and Manuscript Library at Yale University. It is a quarto volume with vellum binding, sewed with four threads, and was formerly fastened with two ties, now missing. On the back of the book, there were originally four square binder's ornaments, but the bottom one is now missing. The pages are 18.5 cm. high and 14 cm. wide. There are 108 numbered pages, in addition to the title page, the dedicatory epistle and poem, and five blank leaves at the beginning.[2] The title, *Divine Meditations*, appears again on page 1 above the poem "The Invocation," and a running head, "Meditations," begins on page 2. The manuscipt is bound in regular gatherings of four from page 1 through page 108.

The gatherings of the introductory material of this manuscript, however, are irregular, and a close examination of them can illuminate the relationship between Colman and Savile. The dedication of this manuscript to Savile was, evidently, a last-minute decision. Both the letter and the single poem to Savile occur in one gathering of leaves, a gathering specially inserted by being pasted to the remnants of two pages cut out of the original volume. Further evidence of Colman's haste lies in the fact that two of these four added leaves are bare; he did not have or take the time to compose dedicatory material to fill the space he added.

The July manuscript was bought by James Osborn in 1951 from Emily Driscoll, who had purchased it the previous year at auction from the earl of Wicklow. Nothing is known about its ownership in the intervening three hundred and ten years.

In preparing the text, I have stayed close to the readings of the manuscripts and have emended as little as possible in order to present an accurate rendering of the existing texts. I have silently expanded the standard abbreviations—for example, "with," "which," "the," "your"—but have preserved Colman's usually consistent substitution of I/i for J/j and his somewhat irregular use of V/v for U/u.

I have made few emendations in punctuation. When one of the manuscripts has even barely appropriate punctuation, I have retained rather

---

2. There are also seven blank leaves at the end of the volume, and a poem, having no connection with Colman's *Divine Meditations*, is written on the sixth leaf in a later hand. I have transcribed this poem in the Appendix as a distinguishing mark of the manuscript.

than modernized it. Therefore, the reader should remember that the concept of punctuation in the seventeenth century differed little from that explained by Richard Puttenham in *The Arte of English Poesie* (1589):

> the very nature of speach (because it goeth by clauses of seuerall construction & sence) requireth some space betwixt them with intermission of sound, to th'end they may not huddle one vpon another so rudly & so fast that th'eare may not perceiue their difference. . . . the auncient reformers of language, inuented, three maner of pauses, one of lesse leasure then another, and such seuerall intermissions of sound to serue (besides easment to the breath) for a treble distinction of sentences or parts of speach, as they happened to be more or lesse perfect in sence. The shortest pause or intermission they called *comma* as who would say a peece of a speach cut of. The second they called *colon*, not a peece but as it were a member for his larger length, because it occupied twise as much time as the *comma*. The third they called *periodus*, for a complement or full pause, and as a resting place and perfection of so much former speach as had bene vttered, and from whence they needed not to passe any further vnles it were to renew more matter to enlarge the tale. This cannot be better represented then by example of these common trauailers by the hie ways, where they seeme to allow themselues three maner of staies or easements: one a horsebacke calling perchaunce for a cup of beere or wine, and hauing dronken it vp rides away and neuer lights: about noone he commeth to his Inne, & there baites him selfe and his horse an houre or more: at night when he can conueniently trauaile no further, he taketh vp his lodging, and rests him selfe till the morrow: from whence he followeth the course of a further voyage, if his businesse be such.[3]

Colman makes extensive use of commas, semicolons, and colons as strong punctuation, and his "voyages" are long ones; for example, lines 5–16 of "A Dreame" (p. 137). Frequently, however, he neglects to write the terminal point when he completes a sentence at the end of a line or a stanza, trusting that his reader will know what should be there. When this omission

3. Richard Puttenham, *The Arte of English Poesie* (London, 1589), pp. 61–62.

occurs and there is no suitable punctuation in the May manuscript, I have supplied the missing period. The preservation of Colman's stylistic freedom is the strongest reason why I have refrained from repunctuating according to the rigid rules of the twentieth century.

BIOGRAPHY

Few facts are known about the life of Henry Colman, the only indisputable ones being that he completed composition of a sequence of religious poems called *Divine Meditations* in 1640 and that two copies of it are extant. The poems are highly intelligent—witty and allusive—and from this I assume that Colman attended either Oxford or Cambridge. It is probable that the author of *Divine Meditations* is the "Henry Coleman" recorded in Venn's *Alumni Cantabrigiensis*,[4] who matriculated as sizar at Trinity College at Easter 1637 and who did not graduate. My assumption that Colman's studies were preparation for ordination is based on the contents of his volume of poetry, despite the fact that many students at the universities chose careers outside the church.[5] No further information is given in the college or university records, for it was not until 1682 that information other than name and status was recorded.[6]

Even Colman's birthplace and home county are unknown. Both copies of *Divine Meditations*, however, are dedicated to men who lived in the West Riding of Yorkshire; therefore, I finally focused my investigations on the historical records of this area. A wide search of Yorkshire records, however, shows only one continuing Colman family, and it lived in the East Riding of Yorkshire near Preston-in-Holderness, relatively distant from the seats of both of Henry Colman's patrons in the southern part of the West Riding. Furthermore, the parish registers at Preston, which have complete records starting in 1559, make no mention of any Colman family member named Henry. Therefore, if one is to know anything more about Henry Colman, one must forego the security

4. John Venn and J. A. Venn, *Alumni Cantabrigiensis* (Cambridge, 1922), 1:369.
5. Mark H. Curtis, *Oxford and Cambridge in Transition 1558–1642* (Oxford, 1959), pp. 61–63.
6. Venn, p. ix.

of concrete fact and venture cautiously into the realm of speculation. I begin with Colman's dedications, for they reveal something of his religious and political allegiances, both in the men to whom he dedicates the volumes and in what he tells about himself in doing so.

In his letter and acrostic to Sir William Savile (*J*), Colman reveals little of himself, only his overwhelming admiration for the high-spirited scion of one of Yorkshire's most prominent families. On his mother's side of the family, Savile was the nephew of Sir Thomas Wentworth, later the earl of Strafford. When Savile was ten years old, his father died, and Sir Thomas became his guardian.[7] Savile was eminent in politics before the Civil Wars; he was elected to the Short Parliament in the spring of 1640,[8] and although he was defeated in his home county in the October elections for the Long Parliament (probably because of the growing unpopularity of his uncle), he did get a place at Old Sarum early in 1641.[9] In spite of Savile's disapproval of some of the king's policies, especially the levying of ship money,[10] he was intensely loyal to the monarchy and to the Anglican church. As Colman rightly praises him,

> L oyaltie in your Princes favour makes you blessd.
> I t is your glory you were thought to be
> A man for wisedome, and for piëtie
> M ost fit to ioyne, your Shiere to rectifie.

> ["Anacrostica," ll. 7–10]

Colman, however, does not claim intimacy with Savile; he says only that he is "one of those farthest from your knowledge, yet ... desire[s] to be knowne ... neere you in my respect." In fact, Henry Colman is

7. For an account of Savile's impetuous rebellion against his uncle's policies, see *The Earl of Strafforde's Letters and Dispatches, with an Essay towards his Life, by Sir George Radcliffe*, ed. William Knowler (Dublin, 1742), 2:215–17, 311, 338–39.

8. Roy Carroll, *The Parliamentary Representation of Yorkshire, 1625–1660* (Ann Arbor, 1964), p. 278; T. D. Whitaker, *Loidis and Elmete* (Leeds, 1816), p. 314; H. C. Foxcroft, *The Life and Letters of Sir George Savile, Bart., First Marquis of Halifax* (London, 1898), 1:12.

9. Carroll, p. 286, n. 37.

10. Samuel Rawson Gardiner, *History of England from the Accession of James to the Outbreak of the Civil War, 1603–1642* (London, 1884), 9:114. Savile made an impassioned speech against ship money on 4 May 1640, the day before Charles I dismissed the Short Parliament.

not mentioned in any of the financial accounts, charities, military appoint-
ments, inventories, personal correspondence, or papers of Sir William
Savile.[11] By the gift of this volume of poetry, his sole asset, Colman
appeals, with little apparent success, to a famous and powerful man for
the opportunity to serve him.

Indeed, it could have been William Rokeby (*M*), who suggested to
the young poet that Sir William Savile might advance his career, for
Rokeby undoubtedly was acquainted with Savile's uncle and guardian,
Sir Thomas Wentworth. Rokeby's home, Skiers Hall in Nether Hoyland,
was within a few miles of Wentworth's estate at Wentworth Woodhouse
and within sight of Holy Trinity Church, where the Wentworth family
worshiped. Colman may well have been a poor tradesman's son, sent to
the university to train for the ministry by his patron Rokeby; consequently, he would not be listed with the eminent or even the socially
interesting persons of the West Riding.

William Rokeby, although less known to the public than Savile, was
also loyal to the monarchy and to the Anglican church. Rokeby's name
is absent from the histories of the period, but he was made a baronet in
1661, the usual reward for political fidelity.[12] The praise that Colman
offers Rokeby is focused, however, not on public political affairs as it
is for Savile, but on Rokeby's personal character. Colman admires
Rokeby's religious orthodoxy amid turmoil and rebellion in the church:

> L earning's depraved, and the sacred Writ
> L ewdly perverted is, and ev'ry wit
> I n selfe-opinion strikes vpon that way
> A lone, that leads to ruine, most doe stray
> M uch from the sincere truth, soe vaine's our clay.
>
> R elligion's made a mocke: soe that to know
> O ne truely great, and good now, is to show
> K nowledge a miracle, . . .
>
> ["Anacrostica Dedicatoria" (II), ll. 3–10]

11. Savile of Rufford Manuscripts (Savile of Thornhill), Nottinghamshire County Record
Office.

12. John Burke and J. B. Burke, *A Genealogical and Heraldic History of the Extinct and Dormant
Baronetcies of England, Ireland, and Scotland*, 2d ed. (London, 1844), p. 452a.

It is obvious from the repeated references to wealth in the dedicatory poems that Rokeby has helped Colman financially, but the value of Rokeby's material gifts becomes negligible when compared with the value of his wise counsel for the young poet.

Colman needed this counsel, for, as his letter to Rokeby mentions, "many late afflictions" had led his "disturbed mind" to the brink of "calamities." He had been attacked by the "mouthes of Calumniators" and by "critticall-Detractour[s]." His only solace had been the support, spiritual as well as financial, of his "honour'd Kinsman, and most approved freind William Rokeby." Colman's "afflictions" may have been the purely personal stresses of one trying to balance the demands of a student's life and a sizar's menial duties with the emergence of his own adult identity. On the other hand, it is possible that challenges were made against his loyalty to the monarchy and to the Anglican church, those loyalties which he held in common with both of his dedicatees. Colman's loyalty to these institutions is clear in his poem "To the Church":

> Hayle, holy Mother of the Christian-band,
> Thou sacred structure of th'Almightie's hand,
> Still may thy honour live, thy beauty be
> Fayre as the best of ages e'r did see;
> May bless'd Peace keepe thee, and thy counsell bringe
> Peace to thy lovers, victory to th'Kinge, . . .
> If any devill seeminge-Christian dare
> Wound thy soft bosome with a traytrous speare,
> Or with pretended zeale defiance bringe
> And prove a schismaticke against the Kinge,
> Or sleight thy reverend Fathers, may they feele
> Thornes in their hearts, or may the iuster steele
> Of faithfull subiects cut them out a lawe,
> Eyther by love, or feare to live in awe,
> Safe be thy sacred treasures, may thy Friend
> Iehovah=Elohim ever defend
> Thy reverend Miters, and their Minor-band,
> And may he please even with his owne right hand
> To blesse with happines, and shield the King

And his race=royall; may thousand Angells bringe
Ayd 'gainst his foes; then shall thy honour live
In spight of all the blowes your foes can give.

[ll. 1–6, 11–26]

The poem is sadly prophetic of the strife of the coming decade.

If Colman was a student at Cambridge, he was close to one focus of the struggle between the monarch and the increasingly Puritan parliament. The House of Commons resented the Crown's exclusive control over the two universities, especially the requirement by James I in 1616 that holders of both superior and inferior degrees subscribe to the three articles —of the supremacy of the king, the *Book of Common Prayer*, and the Articles of Religion—in accordance with Ecclesiastical Canon 36. James held the chancellor and the vice-chancellor of each university (whose election he strongly influenced) responsible for maintaining adherence to all royal proclamations, and he endeavored to insure strict uniformity in religious teaching and practice. Later, Charles I and Archbishop Laud sought to regulate religious life in the universities even more rigidly, making stipulations about instruction.[13] By January 1640/41, only six months after Colman's gift of his poems to Rokeby and Savile, the House of Commons, after much argument, resolved that required subscription "is against the Law and Liberty of the subject and ought not to be pressed upon any student or graduate whatsoever."[14] In fact, in the preceding month, the House of Commons had declared the canons themselves to be illegal.[15]

These conflicts at Cambridge and the loyalty of Colman to church and monarchy may have interrupted his academic progress. The fact is that, for some reason, Colman did not graduate from Cambridge and it is impossible to trace him further.

13. Curtis, pp. 32–34, 171–175.
14. James Heywood and Thomas Wright, *Cambridge University Transactions During the Puritan Controversies of the 16th and 17th Centuries* (London, 1854), 2:438.
15. Gilbert Ainslie, *An Historical Account of the Oaths and Subscriptions Required in the University of Cambridge on Matriculation, and of all Persons who Proceed to the Degree of Master of Arts* (Cambridge, 1833), p. 52.

THE POETRY

Life is surely given us for higher purposes than to gather what our ancestors have wisely thrown away, and to learn what is of no value but because it has been forgotten.

Samuel Johnson

The editor of any unpublished work approaches the task with a mixture of eagerness and skepticism, for Samuel Johnson's pronouncement contains a warning that must be reckoned with. Whether the work is worth preparing and recommending to others depends on what one can gain from reading it—be it information, insight, aesthetic satisfaction, or perhaps all three.

Henry Colman's *Divine Meditations* certainly provides additional information for the scholar. These poems can be used as a measure of the influence of the more prominent poets of the early seventeenth century on the educated, amateur writer, for Colman read broadly and deeply in the poetry of Quarles, Jonson, Donne, and especially Herbert. Furthermore, the poems corroborate much that has been written about the influence of the practice of meditation on seventeenth-century poetry, and they can be advanced as further evidence for the theories of White, Gardner, Martz, and others.[16]

To analyze fully Colman's achievement in *Divine Meditations*, I will first determine the extent of his familiarity with secular and religious literature and then show how the traditions of meditative practice stimulated and directed his insights. Finally, I will consider the thematic unity of *Divine Meditations*, for Colman carefully designed it so that from every perspective it would reflect his understanding of the Christian life. The poems follow the pattern of the Eucharistic liturgy (readings from the Bible, a period for self-examination, the Eucharist itself), and the entire volume emphasizes the fulfillment of the Old Covenant by the

---

16. See Louis L. Martz, *The Poetry of Meditation* (New Haven, 1954); Helen C. White, *English Devotional Literature [Prose] 1600–1640*, University of Wisconsin Studies in Language and Literature, no. 29 (1931); Rosemary Freeman, *English Emblem Books* (London, 1948); *John Donne: The Divine Poems*, ed. Helen Gardner (Oxford, 1952); *The Sonnets of William Alabaster*, ed. Helen Gardner and G. M. Story (London, 1959).

New. Colman sees this large schema as parallel to the development of his own relationship with God as he, metaphorically, leaves the wandering exile of self-ignorance to reclaim his true identity as the child of God by recovering the Divine Image in which he was originally created.

The Literary Context

Colman's poetry shows the influence of the poetry, religious and secular, of the late sixteenth and early seventeenth centuries. In *Divine Meditations*, we hear both metrical and verbal echoes of this poetry, for his ear has caught the rhythms and phrases of his literary environment. The most important sources of influence on Colman's poetry are Quarles's *Emblemes*, the poems of Ben Jonson and of John Donne, and especially George Herbert's *The Temple*. As we shall see, Colman read widely and borrowed boldly, but he is seldom merely derivative. He has a creative, as well as an assimilative mind, and his *Divine Meditations* is an independent poetic achievement.

Divine Meditations contains a variety of metrical and stanzaic patterns, and this variety reveals much about the extent of Colman's reading. In Quarles's *Emblemes* we find one of the stanzaic patterns that Colman uses most frequently, the pronounced alternation between long and short lines. For an extreme example, we may note *Emblemes* I, 6 and II, 14, in which pentameter and dimeter lines alternate. Colman borrows this form for "On God's Mercie" (p. 72), "On Mortalitie" (p. 75), "Another [On Drunckenesse]" (p. 104), "On Beautie" (p. 107), "On his Birth-day" (p. 127), and "On Lazarus rais'd from death" (p. 110). Colman's "On Death" (p. 99) uses another of Quarles's stanzas, the rhyming three-line stanza of *Emblemes* III, 7, 12, and 13, and IV, 13; Colman uses an iambic tetrameter line, however, instead of Quarles's iambic pentameter lines. Colman's use of the pentameter couplet in such poems as "Another [On Christ's Passion]" (p. 80), "To the Church" (p. 134), "A Dreame" (p. 137), and "On Povertie" (p. 141) often resembles Jonson's use of it; its mobile caesura and frequent enjambment lend to these meditations the colloquial familiarity that we find in Jonson's "Epistle to Katherine, Lady Aubigny" or "To Penshurst."

Another Jonsonian cadence that Colman uses is the trochaic tetrameter couplet, in which Jonson wrote many of the songs in his plays and masques as well as seven of the ten poems in "The Celebration of CHARIS." Jonson takes the meter, of course, from the long tradition of the Elizabethan lyric, in which it was used by Shakespeare, Campion, Wither, and many others. Lest readers associate the meter with love lyrics alone, they should note that it was used for other types of poems as well: for example, Jonson's "Epitaph on Elizabeth, L. H." and Samuel Daniel's "Are they shadows that we see?" from *Tethys Festival* (1610). Colman uses this meter for "On Immortalitie" (p. 79), "Another [On Prayer]" (p. 98), and "On his Birth. A Pastorall" (p. 125). The variety of metrical and stanzaic forms in Colman's *Divine Meditations* reflects most obviously the variety found in *The Temple* of Herbert. Colman, indeed, imitates the virtuosity of Herbert, but since form and content are so closely intertwined in *The Temple*, a discussion of Colman's technical debt to Herbert will be postponed until the discussion of *The Temple* as a whole (pp. 20ff).

When the verbal influence of these poets on *Divine Meditations* is considered, Colman's independence and artistry become plain. Colman does not hesitate to acquire a subject, a situation, a phrase, or even a line or two from another poet. As if to compensate for this sometimes conspicuous reliance on others, he strips away the superfluous, he elaborates the simplistic, and he transforms the secular into the devotional. For all his youthful dependence on earlier poets, Colman displays wit that makes up for his obligations.

The economy which is characteristic of many of Colman's poems is most apparent in those that germinated from Quarles's overblown, though immensely popular, verse. For example, contrast the "Invocation" of Quarles's *Emblemes* with that of Colman's *Divine Meditations*. Both poets ask the inspiration of God alone for their efforts, but Colman's poem succinctly formulates in ten lines the same plea that Quarles lards to forty-eight lines. Colman writes:

> I invocate noe Nymph, noe Grace, noe Muse
> To helpe my wit, I vtterly refuse
> All such fond aides, and call vpon thy name

> Alone, ô God t'inspire me with a flame
> Terse, and sublime; that whatsoe'r I write
> May season'd be by thy diviner Sp'rite;
> Inspire my barren fancy, and distill
> Such sacred matter through my feeble quill
> That ev'ry line I write thy name may raise,
> And every leafe may celebrate thy praise.

The main tropes of Colman's poem are imbedded in Quarles's, and in only twelve lines excerpted from Quarles's "Invocation" we find the inspiration for Colman's poem and the meat of Quarles's. Quarles speaks first to his soul:

> Invoke no Muse; Let heav'n be thy *Apollo*;
> And let his sacred Influences hallow
> Thy high-bred Straynes; Let his full beames inspire
> Thy ravisht braines with more heroick fire;
>   . . . and let heav'ns fire season
> The fresh Conceits of thy corrected Reason.[17]

Then he appeals to God ("Thou great Theanthropos"):

> Enrich my Fancy, clarifie my thoughts,
> Refine my drosse, O, wink at humane faults;
> And through this slender Conduit of my Quill,
> Convey thy Current, whose cleare streames may fill
> The hearts of men with love, their tongues with praise;
> Crowne me with Glory: Take, who list, the Bayes.

>   [ll. 43–48]

The remaining lines of Quarles's "Invocation" consist of inflation of these lines by lengthy parallelisms. Colman has borrowed what was pertinent to his need, and his prayer for a "Terse" flame of inspiration seems to have been answered.

Colman's sequence of eight poems about "judgment" (pp. 88–96) seems to derive from Quarles's rather simple *psychomachia* at the Day of

---

17. Francis Quarles, *Emblemes* (London, 1635), pp. 1–2. All further quotations will be taken from this edition.

Judgment, in which Jesus and Justice quarrel about the fate of a sinner (*Emblemes*, III, 10). Colman's version, however, displays a more complex understanding of the psychology of the sinner than Quarles's does, as well as a richly witty play with two contexts of judgment—the final judgment which precedes the heavenly banquet in the New Jerusalem (Quarles's *only* meaning) and, in the context of his volume's patterning on the Eucharistic liturgy, the self-examination of the potential communicant before he receives the sacrament. In spite of the overtly dramatic beginning —the cry of "o yes" [*oyez*] as a court official would announce the opening of the traveling court—the poems, named for steps in the judicial process, present action that is internal, all of the events occurring within the meditating mind of the poet. In following St. Bernard's instruction to "place all thy transgressions before thy eyes: place thy selfe before thy selfe, as it were before another, and so bewaile thy selfe,"[18] the poet becomes the complete judicial system—defendant, jury, and judge—and knows from the start that he is guilty. In "The Summons," the defendant, called "sinfull flesh" already, is told that he "will find/ Most favour by confession," and in "The Arraignment" he is addressed as "sinfull soule" and told to "lay thy guilty hand" on the bar of justice. After a stern voice reads "The Indictment" (which follows the orthodox categories of sin: original sin, the seven mortal sins, sins of omission, sins of commission, plus "thousand thousands more"), we hear the pleas of the "regenerate sinner" and the "unregenerate sinner," pleas which portray the poet's conflicting desires: first, admitting his faults, to bear his punishment and, second, proclaiming his many good works, to escape. The verdict and the sentence follow in quasi-judicial order, and "The Appendixe" finally states explicitly that the judgment scene is an interior one:

> Conscience th'Accuser is
> Who in this Triall
> Will all excuses misse,
> Take noe denyall.
>
> [ll. 7–10]

---

18. St. Bernard of Clairvaux, *Saint Bernard His Meditations*, 4th ed. (London, 1631–32), pt. 2, p. 48.

The various tones of voice in the drama—accusing, confessing, pleading, whining, sentencing—reflect the poet's diverse impulses as he confronts his sins and suggest dimensions of psychological insight absent from Quarles's judgment drama.

Colman even uses Quarles's typical structure, the emblem, in composing his meditations. The standard form of the emblematic meditation is an allegorical picture followed by a poem that explains the significance of the picture. The picture gives visual form to the subject of the meditation and supplies the meditator with a concrete focus for his attention, while the poem analyzes the picture and ends with a succinct moral. Colman uses the emblematic method in conjunction with other, more subtle methods of meditation. His poem "Another [On Death]" (p. 100) is the most strictly emblematic of his poems, but as one of a series of poems about death, it has a special function: it presents the subject vividly to the meditator. The first poem of the series, "On Death" (p. 99), abstractly introduces the subject of death and the fragility of mortal life; its last stanza exhorts the poet to consider his tenuous hold on life and to prepare for death:

> Let vs then prepared be
> To meete death when'ever he
> Shall call vs to eternitie.
>
> [ll. 16–18]

"Another" begins this preparation of the mind for consideration of death by comparing death to its counterpart, sleep. The poem is a meticulous compilation of common similitudes:

> My bed's my grave, my grave's my bed,
> My sleepe's like death, I sleepe but dead; . . .
> My sheets I sleepe in seeme to me
> Nought but my windinge-sheet to be.
> When I am layd downe in my bed,
> Me-thinks I then seeme coffined.
>
> [ll. 1–2, 9–12]

The last couplet of the poem states the method and the purpose of this form of meditation:

> And each thinge in a severall fashion
> Presents death to my meditation.

[ll. 15–16]

Here Colman admits the limitations of the emblematic method; for him, it is useful only as the prelude to meditation, that portion of the exercise in which he summons the images that represent his subject concretely to his analytic faculty. The extent of Colman's debt to Quarles shown in these poems is, I think, an accurate measure of Quarles's influence on *Divine Meditations* in general. Certainly, Colman was thoroughly familiar with Quarles's *Emblemes*, but he resorted to Quarles's most typical form only once and was not limited by his verbal style.

As a rule, Colman sought more flexible forms than the emblem and indulged his flair for wit, pun, and paradox more freely than did the somber Quarles. This flair emerges in "On the life of Christ" (p. 123), Colman's imitation of Ben Jonson's "Ode Allegorical" which prefaced Hugh Holland's *Pancharis* (1603). Jonson's conventional compliment to Holland is a laborious comparison of a fellow-poet to a "black swan," while Colman's description of Christ as a "black swan" wittily explores the paradox of the Incarnation.

The metaphor common to both poems is the comparison of the subject of the poem to a "black swan," a proverbial term in the sixteenth and seventeenth centuries for something extremely rare or even nonexistent; the phrase comes from Juvenal's Satire 6, "The Ways of Women," in which he says that a wife who is beautiful, rich, fertile, and chaste is as "rare a bird on earth as is a black swan" (*rara avis in terris nigroque simillima cycno*: 6. 165). Jonson uses the image to distinguish Holland from the common race of "swans" or poets. Holland's "feathers" are black because Phoebus Apollo burns them with his lovingly protective rays ("From Zephyr's rape would close him with his beames,")[19] but his breast (figur-

---

19. *Ben Jonson*, ed. C. H. Herford, Percy and Evelyn Simpson, 11 vols. (Oxford, 1925–52), 8:366, l. 24. All further quotations will be taken from this edition.

atively, his soul or heart) remains white. Jonson then traces the black swan's journey throughout the British Isles (probably as an allegory of Holland's trip to the Continent), endows him with eternity by transmuting him into the celestial constellation Cygnus, and concludes that no river in the world ever "can/Set out a like, or second to our Swan" (ll. 119–20). Colman's poem follows the general pattern of Jonson's: justification of the metaphor of the "black swan," allegorization of the important events in the subject's life, and explanation of the circumstances of his apotheosis. Colman's verbal play, however, engages the mind with a theme of theological significance, as he uses the image of the black swan—the *rara avis*, both "faire" and "black," at home in both air and water—to describe the twofold nature of Christ.

The first stanza of the poem presents the paradox: in answer to the question of whether a black swan ever existed, Colman replies that

> Poore Beth'lem did produce
> A bird more faire
> Then any water, Rivulet, or sluce
> E'r knew, the ayre
> Never was beate by any winge could showe
> Such heavenly beauty as this bird did owe.
>
> [ll. 3–8]

But what is the connection of this "faire" bird to the "blacke swan" introduced in the second line of the poem? The second stanza clarifies the paradox:

> This faire one from above tooke flight,
> And is i'th'breast more white
> Then e'r was any Swan.
> That part nor wind,
> Nor sunne, nor any foule infection can
> Make t'alter kind.
>
> [ll. 9–14]

Colman plays on both the figurative and the literal meanings of "breast," as did Jonson, to create a moment of confusion before the figurative meaning (heart, soul) asserts itself: figuratively, the black swan's "breast" is "faire" and "white," and reflects its spiritual essence, purity and innocence, in contrast to its physical color, black. Although "This faire one from above" has taken the physical appearance of a black swan (blackness denotes his "defilement" by material form as well as his rarity), his breast (the essentially divine nature of his soul) can be altered neither by forces of the natural world ("nor wind,/ Nor sunne"—lines 12–13) nor by actual existence in the physical world as one of its creatures. Not even "foule infection," Colman's punning description of Christ's incarnation as a bird, can change the essential divinity of Christ, "can/ Make t'alter kind"; indeed, only by this conjunction of his immutable divinity with creaturely form can the swan (Christ) become the sacrifice and atonement for sins and, therefore, the "altar kind," the holy species of the Eucharistic meal. The pun "foule infection" is conscious on Colman's part, for it is the only change he makes in the lines from Jonson's poem included in his. Jonson writes of the breast of his swan, Holland,

> That part nor Winde,
> Nor Sunne could make to vary from the rest,
> Or alter kinde.

> [ll. 28–30]

Colman substitutes his pun, which describes the Incarnation in terms of the dominant image, in place of Jonson's half-line, which merely duplicates the information of the following line. After these two stanzas, which grapple with the paradox, we know that the black swan is the incarnate Christ and can enjoy the simpler development of this analogy that Colman accomplishes with ingenuity and persistence in the remainder of the poem.

The spiritual presence of John Donne is clearly felt in Colman's poetry. As Dean of St. Paul's Cathedral and frequent preacher to James I and Charles I, Donne was an eminent churchman during Colman's youth. Many of his sermons were published and the two *Anniversaries* were frequently reprinted between 1611 and 1640. Although the bulk of Donne's poetry ("Songs and Sonets," "Holy Sonnets" and other religious poems, complimentary and occasional verse, elegies, epistles) was published in 1633 and 1639, Colman is more strongly influenced by the *Anniversaries*;

his poems echo them verbally and thematically (see "Commentary"). His most obvious derivation from these two poems is the praise of the dedicatee as a figure of nearly divine stature. Both Elizabeth Drury and William Rokeby are portrayed as principles of order, with goodness beyond the merely human, while Donne and Colman define themselves as the unworthy beneficiaries of those exemplary lives and as the chroniclers of their virtue. Comparison of texts and specific discussion of this influence are reserved for the discussion of Colman's dedicatory material (pp. 38–39).

Colman absorbed much from the religious and the literary practices of his time, and these two strains of influence join in the most important source of inspiration for *Divine Meditations*, George Herbert's *The Temple*. Published for the first time in 1633, *The Temple* was immediately popular and influential; five editions had been published by 1640 and its imitators were numerous. Christopher Harvey published *The Synagogue, or, The Shadow of the Temple* anonymously in 1640, and from its second edition in 1647 on, it was bound in the same volume with Herbert's poems. *The Synagogue* was followed by Richard Crashaw's *Steps to the Temple* (1646), by Mildmay Fane's *Otia Sacra* (1648), and by Henry Vaughan's *Silex Scintillans* (1650, 1655) which echoes Herbert's poems endlessly. Colman's volume shows how carefully studied and sensitively understood *The Temple* was by a contemporary reader, and the pervasive influence of *The Temple* on *Divine Meditations* makes probable the identification of its author with the "Henry Coleman" who matriculated at Trinity College in 1637. This "Henry Coleman" studied in Herbert's own college (where he had been a fellow and sublector) at the university in which Herbert had been praelector in rhetoric and official orator. Herbert's poems, published by the university press, would have been especially known and honored there.[20] In "The Printers to the Reader" (a preface written by Nicholas Ferrar and found in all printed editions from 1633 to 1695),

---

20. In "Directions for a Student in the Universitie," a manuscript (MS. 48) in the Library of Emmanuel College, Cambridge, Herbert's *Poems* is one of the contemporary works suggested. The evidence is strong that the original version of the "Directions" was written by Richard Holdsworth while he was a fellow of St. John's College from 1613 to 1620. Ms. 48 is a revision of Holdsworth's work, updated with additional titles by later generations of tutors. See Curtis, pp. 133, 289–90.

Herbert is lauded as a "companion to the primitive Saints, and a pattern
. . . for the age he lived in."[21] For Colman, Herbert became both a spiritual
pattern and a literary master—the ground from which Colman's own
achievement would spring.

We see the impress of Herbert's style and spirit on Colman's volume
both in content and in form. *Divine Meditations* frequently echoes *The
Temple* verbally, as the commentary on this edition makes plain. Both
volumes are the "first-fruits" of their authors' minds (see Herbert's "The
Dedication" and Colman's letters of dedication), and Colman also imitates
many of the types of poems that we find in *The Temple*. The most conspicuous imitation, of course, is "The Altar," the opening poem in the
main part of *The Temple*, the "Church," and the second poem in Colman's
volume. There are, moreover, other pairs of similar poems in the two
volumes: for example, Herbert's "Easter-wings" (p. 43) and Colman's
"On Prayer" (p. 97)—wing-shaped poems in which the wings offer a
way for the poet or his prayers to go to Heaven; Herbert's "The Quip"
(p. 110) and Colman's "On my enemies vniust malice" (p. 73)—poems
of imprecation; Herbert's "Heaven" (p. 188) and Colman's "Another
[On Death]" (p. 101)—echo poems which affirm the existence of Heaven;
Herbert's "A Parodie" (p. 183) and Colman's "On Drunckenesse" (p. 103)
—parodies of secular love lyrics;[22] Herbert's "The Invitation" (p. 179)
and "The Banquet" (p. 181) and Colman's "The Invitation" (p. 131) and
"On the Lords Supper" (p. 132)—sequences about the Eucharist and the
Feast of the Saints in Heaven, which are placed close to the end of each
volume. In short, these correlative poems sum up a considerable debt to
Herbert.

Other types of poems common to both poets are the acrostic and the
anagram, forms which Herbert invigorates with subtlety, while Colman's
use of them is admittedly commonplace. In both the acrostic and the

21. George Herbert, *The Works of George Herbert*, ed. F. E. Hutchinson, 2d ed. (Oxford,
1964), p. 3. All quotations from Herbert's works are taken from this edition.

22. Herbert's poem derives from "Soules joy, now I am gone" which Grierson attributes
to the earl of Pembroke, not to Donne, as had been thought previously; Colman's poem
parodies Thomas Carew's "Song: Eternitie of love protested," which begins "How ill doth
he deserve the name of lover." See *The Poems of Thomas Carew with his Masque "Coelum
Britannicum,"* ed. Rhodes Dunlap (Oxford, 1949), p. 23.

anagram, the letters of a name are specially placed in order to reveal a "hidden" meaning. Herbert does this in his "Anagram of the Virgin Marie" (p. 77); Colman uses the acrostic for his dedicatory poems and combines it skillfully with the anagram in his third dedicatory poem to William Rokeby.

Both poets use these forms most significantly for their meditations on the name of Jesus. Both Herbert and Colman "hide" the letters of Jesus' name in acrostics and anagrams, and in the poems that result from these spelling games, the verbal playfulness is a means of revelation. In Herbert's "Lovejoy" (p. 116), the "J" and "C" "anneal'd on every bunch" of grapes are, of course, the initials of Jesus Christ, but the speaker's "Judgement" of the puzzle is also correct, for "Joy" and "Charitie" are essential to Jesus' nature. The constancy of Jesus is revealed in Herbert's anagram "Jesu" (p. 112). Even when the speaker's heart (on which the name "Jesu" is "deeply carved") is broken by affliction, Jesus continues to be a source of comfort, for the fragments of the broken heart (bearing the letters (I, ES, and U) spell "I ease you."

Colman uses only the acrostic for his meditations on Jesus' name. "On the names Iesus, Christ, Emanuell" (p. 109) makes the names the shaping principle of the poem, and the lines that are attached to the letters in the names elaborate the significance of those names. Jesus is the Christ, the anointed one who is the balm (chrism) for the "fester'd heart" of the "sinsicke world." Jesus is also Emanuell, in Hebrew—"God with us"; for only God can cure man's sinsickness, and Jesus is the manifestation of God in this world. The lines of the poem express the meanings of the names, and conversely, the names themselves seem to be pressed out of the poem, as oil from a seed, to stand alone in marked significance. Colman's second acrostic on the name of Jesus, "On the Inscription over the head of Christ on the Cross" (pp. 146–47), is more elaborate than the first, for it is a double acrostic; that is, both ends spell out "Iesus of Nazareth the King of the Iewes." This poem presents a more complex portrait of Jesus, for Jesus speaks from the cross in the voice of the omnipotent redeemer. His physical position shows the suffering of the incarnate God, but his words proclaim his power to overcome the world; the double use of Jesus' name and title to form the poem signifies his twofold nature. Herbert is clearly the adept master in the use of these mechanical devices for shaping a poem, and Colman, his earnest student.

Both Colman's independence and his imitation of Herbert can be seen in their poems each entitled "The Altar." In addition to the similar shapes of the poems, each is a poem of praise to God. Furthermore, each poem is an introduction: Herbert's introduces "The Church," the complex lyric middle section of *The Temple*, and Colman's introduces his entire volume of poetry. As introductory poems, they point out the focus of each volume and thus provide the reader with insight into the pattern of the poems that follow. A comparison of the poems, however, reveals a significant difference between them in the tone in which the praise is offered, and this difference characterizes the two volumes in their entirety.

Herbert's "Altar" acknowledges the rigor and the sometimes agonizing struggle of the Christian life. Only by constructing his heart in the physical form of sacrificial praise can the poet be certain that his heart will always praise God. Herbert emphasizes the hardness of the building material of his altar (stone), which he finds an all-too-frequently apt analogy for the essence of his heart.

> A HEART alone
> Is such a stone,
> As nothing but
> Thy pow'r doth cut.
> Wherefore each part
> Of my hard heart
> Meets in this frame,
> To praise thy Name:
> That, if I chance to hold my peace,
> These stones to praise thee may not cease.
>
> [ll. 5–14]

Herbert's "Altar" is the poem of a man who knows and abhors, but is resigned to, his own recalcitrance. In his account of the unity of *The Temple*, Martz has defined three stages of the spiritual journey in "The Church": first, the affirmation of the redemption of sinners as shown in the Passion and in the sacraments of the church; second, the "spiritual combat," in which Herbert's speaker suffers recurrent cycles of affliction, growth, and comprehension in learning to accept the gift of redemption; and third, the hard-won "plateau of assurance" where the speaker has, at last, humbled himself and made himself ready to receive the sacrament's healing and comfort.[23] On the "plateau of assurance," however, the speaker's certainty fluctuates, though never as violently as in the second section, and we note hesitance and remorse even in the final poem of "The Church," "Love" (III). The struggle in the soul between its aspirations and its inclinations is painfully evident in Herbert's "Altar" and is the theme repeated throughout "The Church."

Colman's poem, on the other hand, does not have the grim resolution of Herbert's; instead, we find a repentance that the speaker trusts to be pure and acceptable to God. It is interesting to look at the biblical text which is the basis for both poems, Exodus 20:24–25, and to notice the different emphases of Herbert and Colman.

> An altar of earth thou shalt make unto me, and shalt sacrifice thereon thy burnt offerings, and thy peace offerings, thy sheep, and thine oxen: in all places where I record my name I will come unto thee, and I will bless thee. And if thou wilt make me an altar of stone, thou shalt not build it of hewn stone: for if thou lift up thy tool upon it, thou hast polluted it.

Herbert pessimistically assumes his altar, or heart, to be made from stone, the harder substance, whereas Colman assumes his to be made of clay, the common material of all human beings as well as altars. The constitution of Colman's heart is implicit in lines 3 and 4; it is "Humble" ("clay, dirt" from L. *humus*), "contrite" ("crushed, ground to a powder" from L. *contero*), yet bound together by the water of tears and shaped by sighs and sobs of repentance. It is also "free" (line 2) and glad to be formed into an altar for the offering of praise. The peaceful quietness of sins forgiven and the sinner accepted infuses Colman's poem, and this difference in emphasis characterizes the different "plot" of Colman's volume. In contrast to Herbert's "The Altar," which introduced a history of spiritual conflict,

---

23. Martz, pp. 288–320.

Colman's "The Altar" is written by a healthy, vital member of Christ's body and introduces meditations arranged in an order that shows the means by which the poet has attained this health, the liturgy of the Eucharist.

Obviously, the strongest literary influence on Colman comes from contemporary religious poets—Quarles, Donne, and Herbert. The religious matrix shared by them all is the meditative tradition; it provides a structural and a thematic background against which we can see Colman's unique accomplishment clearly.

The Meditative Tradition

The title that Henry Colman chose for his volume of poetry, *Divine Meditations*, immediately associates it with other books of poetry in his era that are influenced by that special form of prayer or devotional discipline known as meditation. In three early manuscripts, John Donne's *Holy Sonnets* are entitled *Divine Meditations*,[24] and Colman read the popular religious poems of Francis Quarles, the *Divine Fancies* (1632) and the *Emblemes* (1635), which make elementary use of meditative principles. Indeed, by the middle third of the seventeenth century, the practice of meditation, in a more or less formal way, was a standard poetic technique as well as a commonplace of religious duty.

Meditation, an ancient religious exercise, is an attempt to stimulate devotion and to encourage righteous action by arousing the imagination to an intense, personal awareness of religious issues and events, particularly the events and consequences of the life of Christ. As St. Bernard explains in the "Epistle Dedicatorie" to his meditations on the Passion:

> I haue much endeauoured, so to expresse the grieuous Passion of our gracious Redeemer, as if it were now in present action before our eyes, that I might the better stirre vp feruent motions of Pietie in the mind, and kindle the sparkes of true deuotion in the heart of the Reader. For indeed, the full scope of my desire is to glorifie God, and benefit my brethren.
>
> And as in matter of sorrow, it more deeply pierceth the soule of the

24. *John Donne: The Divine Poems*, ed. Helen Gardner (Oxford, 1952), p. xxxix.

hearer with griefe or in matter of delight, more affecteth the minde
with ioy, to heare the particular relation of some Tragical euent, or the
parts and particles of some delightfull accident reported then onely
to heare a bare narration of either in grosse, without expressing the
parts thereof: so likewise it cannot chuse, but more deepely wound the
soule of euery Christian, to heare, or read the speciall and seuerall
sufferings of Christ in his Passion, then if it were onely sayd thus,
Christ died for vs.[25]

St. Ignatius Loyola's *Spiritual Exercises*, composed in 1526, systematized
this method of prayer by concentrating the three powers of the soul—
memory, understanding, and will—on one subject. In a typical Ignatian
meditation, the memory is applied to the chosen subject in the "composition of place" to bring forward all that the meditator has known or
can imagine about it. Next, the understanding analyzes the subject, point
by point; there are usually three or five points for consideration. Finally,
the third power of the soul, the will, draws conclusions, which prompt
an outpouring of devotion aroused in the course of the meditation;
usually, this outpouring takes the form of a colloquy with God in which
the meditator vows to amend his life and to apply his new insights to his
own situation.

Loyola designed this method of devotion as a way of testing men who
wanted to dedicate their entire lives, private and professional, to the
Jesuit order. At the beginning of the seventeenth century, however, there
was a reaction against the rigor of the *Exercises*, and spiritual leaders, such
as St. Francis de Sales, modified the method to enrich the spiritual life of
the secular layperson.[26] St. Francis de Sales directs his *Introduction to a
Deuoute Life* to "such as liue in citties and townes, busied with the affaires
of their houshold, or forced by their place and calling to folow their
princes court, such as by the obligation of their estate, are bound to take a
common course of life in outward shew, and exterior proceeding."[27]

25. *Saint Bernard His Meditations*, pt. 1, sigs. A₄–A₅v.

26. Martz, p. 56.

27. *An Introduction to a Deuoute Life, Composed in Frenche By the R. Father in God Francis
Sales, Bishop of Geneua, and Translated into English by I[ohn] Y[akesley]*, 3d ed. (Rouen, 1614),
pp. 10–12.

Adapted for the Christian's life in the world, such directions for gentle exercise of the spirit became the staple of the prose devotional manuals. For example, consider the instruction of George Webbe in his contribution to A GARDEN *of Spirituall Flowers* (1630), "How to behaue our selues in solitarinesse":

> When thou art free from company, and in solitarinesse alone by thy selfe, haue a care that . . . thy thoughts be not ranging or wandring, but kept within compasse: Be frequent at such time in diuine Meditations, and Soliloquies vnto God, redeeming the time to the best vse that thou canst.[28]

Such carefully planned use of the leisure that a Christian enjoys in his secular occupation is thus part of every Christian's duty. Colman says that his *Divine Meditations* is the fruit of the leisure hours of his life as a student, hours that he spent in meditation—his *Horae successivae*, as he calls them, perhaps after the book of brief meditations by Joseph Henshaw that he probably used as a guide in his devotions.

But what is the main influence of these traditional forms of meditation on poetry, especially on Colman's volume? Primarily, as Martz says, traditional meditation "brings together the senses, the emotions, and the intellectual faculties of man . . . in a moment of dramatic, creative experience."[29] Meditation stimulates the mind of the poet and concentrates it on a single subject; the poetry that may result is a distillation of the insights and emotions gained in the course of the exercise. As Colman says in his letter to Rokeby, he "digested" some of the thoughts resulting from his meditations "into writinge, even in the shape (except a little more rough-cast) that I now present them you." Meditation, then, is a process by which the materials of poetry are marshaled in the mind of the meditator; whether poetry is produced depends on his temper and his talent.

Colman uses many of the traditional techniques of meditation in the composition of *Divine Meditations*. As a poet, he finds one of the most useful aspects of the meditative process to be the potential drama of a scene

---

28. George Webbe, *A GARDEN of Spirituall Flowers* (London, 1630), sigs. G_1, G_1v.
29. Martz, p. 1.

when it is presented vividly in the theatre of the mind by the memory and imagination. He uses this potential drama both objectively—in the exemplary poems, where the speaker is a biblical character and bears no trace of the identity of the meditator himself—and subjectively—in those poems where the speaker imagines himself a part of the scene being dramatized.

The exemplary poems of *Divine Meditations* present the ideal to which the struggling Christian aspires but which the meditator has not yet attained. Because he cannot yet identify with this ideal, Colman creates a totally dramatic context. "On his Birth. A Pastorall" (p. 125) is a playlet in which the Wise Men meet the shepherds on their way to worship the newborn Jesus. Colman stresses the disparity in their social rank, shown in their diction and attitudes, but this disparity is transcended by their common desire to find the Christ Child. The poem contains no colloquy, for to do so would be a transgression of its dramatic integrity. Equally impersonal is the dramatic monologue, "On Lazarus, rais'd from death" (p. 110), in which Lazarus's account of his return from the grave shows vividly the healing power of Jesus, which was described in the preceding poem, "On the names Iesus, Christ, Emanuell." The speaker throughout the poem is Lazarus, and Colman does not play a role in this meditation. It and "On his Birth. A Pastorall" provide vignettes of the perfections which the poet contemplates. These dramatic poems are frequently part of a series which forms an extended meditation on one subject; other poems in such a series present aspects of the meditative process in which the poet takes a direct role.

Colman's *Divine Meditations* also contains poems in which the poet participates directly in the dramatization of the meditative subject. If he finds a biblical situation that duplicates his own, he blends his voice with the voice of the protagonist in that situation. In "On my enemies vniust malice," for example, the afflictions of the beleaguered psalmist are so like his own that both he and the psalmist can bewail their troubles in unison. Sometimes, on the other hand, the poet, in his contemporaneity, imagines himself present at the biblical scene that he is dramatizing. In the meditations on the Crucifixion, for example, the poet, as a seventeenth-century meditator, is part of the tableau on Calvary and the Via

Dolorosa. In "On Christ's Passion" (p. 80), Colman accuses himself of every injury to Jesus, realizing that his sins are the thorns and the scourge, and that he himself is the "graceles wretch [who] betray'd his gracious Lord" (line 1) as well as the "Soldier that did pierce his side" (line 11). In "Another [On Christ's Passion]," we see more forceful interaction between the meditator and the scene he meditates on. The poem shows dramatically the changes that the careful analysis of the scene makes in the mind of the poet. We hear first the words of Jesus as he submits to the indignities of the preliminaries to his crucifixion:

> . . . I am nigh
> To all that truely seeke me: But what rage
> Hath forc'd you arm'd to seeke me? disingage
> Your better iudgments, and you'l quickly find
> I never was to Penitents vnkind. . . .
> . . . Well, behold I goe
> Whither you'l leade me, though I could have showne
> My might, and Angells to my ayd call'd downe.

> [ll. 2–6, 12–14]

The spectator-poet, for the next fifty-eight lines, harangues those who were present: the "wicked rout," Herod, the scribes and priests, Pilate, Simon of Cyrene, those who actually nailed Christ to the cross, and the two thieves. It is only after Jesus speaks a second time that the meditator sees how his own sins have caused the sufferings of Jesus. Jesus says

> O cruell hearts can you (for all this) se
> Me thus tormented for your sinnes, and ye
> And not afford me pittie? knowe that none
> Ever such sorrow felt as I have knowne,
> Yea even the fiercenes of my Fathers ire,
> For nothinge lesse your scarlet crimes require.

> [ll. 73–78]

Jesus' description of his sufferings, especially the ultimate alienation from God his Father, moves the meditator to an eloquent colloquy, in which he turns his criticism against himself.

> And is all this for me,! and shall I dare
> To se thee thus, and not let fall one teare
> For thee, and for my sinnes? O graunt thy grace
> That they may trickle from my heart apace,
> And never stint, till by the bloud of thee
> I am made Cleane from my impuritie.

[ll. 79–84]

A measure of the meditator's awareness of his own sinfulness is the frequency of first-person pronouns in these lines, six references to himself in as many lines, in contrast to the total absence of them in his previous fifty-eight-line tirade. These two poems about the Crucifixion show variations of the meditative technique of placing oneself in the midst of the proposed situation. In the first, an emotionally static poem, we hear only the colloquy, the passionate conclusion of the meditation. The second poem is more complex, for it recapitulates the several attitudes of the poet during the course of the meditation; it shows the dawning of understanding rather than simply a state of contrition.

The prime requisite for development of the devotional life is self-knowledge, and the meditative tradition prescribes techniques to help the meditator gain a sure understanding of who he is. The medieval theologians, and St. Ignatius as well, provided for this fundamental step in their counsel. St. Bernard posits three dimensions of human identity, each a necessary corrective to the other two: first, the fact of humanity's pre-eminence in the natural world; second, humanity's awareness of this pre-eminent rank; third, the knowledge that this pre-eminence is the gift of God and that human beings are not the source of their own greatness.[30] Only when the meditator sees himself in this cosmic context can he progress in his relationship with God. St. Ignatius, in the sixteenth century, stipulates that the meditations of the first week of his *Exercises* be "designed to arouse a sense of the fearful necessity of self-knowledge."[31] Some subjects that St. Ignatius suggests for these initial meditations are sin, death,

---

30. Etienne Gilson, *The Mystical Theology of St. Bernard*, trans. A. H. C. Downes (New York, 1940), pp. 34–35.
31. Martz, p. 124.

Hell, judgment, and the Prodigal Son, as well as a detailed, categorical self-examination in light of the Ten Commandments, the seven deadly sins, and the five senses. Colman uses many of these techniques in *Divine Meditations*. Sin is his subject in "On the Spirit adulterated by the flesh" (p. 87), and he considers specific sins in the two poems "On Drunckenesse" (pp. 103, 104), in "On Anger" (p. 108), and "On Pride" (p. 118). In Colman's sequence of eight poems dramatizing the soul's trial on Judgment Day (pp. 88–96; discussed above, pp. 14–16), "The Indictment" is organized according to orthodox categories of sins.

The "most widely and intensely cultivated" means to self-knowledge, as Martz points out,[32] is the meditation on death, which illuminates, as nothing else can, one's place in the cosmic context. Acknowledgment of the fragility of flesh and the temporariness of accomplishments in the natural world readies one to accept God's grace by teaching the finitude of human identity. Colman's meditations on death amply illustrate these goals. Death is the title of three poems (pp. 99, 100, 101) and the subject of "On the names Iesus, Christ, Emanuell" (p. 109), "On Lazarus rais'd from death" (p. 110), and "My last will, and Testament" (p. 112). In the first three poems, Colman emphasizes the omnipresence of death and humanity's constant vulnerability. He dwells with grisly concentration on the naturalistic aspects of death:

> The more I thinke, the more I may,
> How soone we passe from hence away
> To people graves, how fraile's our clay.
>
> A thousand wayes we have from hence,
> Against the smallest worme noe fence
> Can save vs from Deaths residence.
>
> ["On Death," ll. 1–6]
>
> Why to our clay was life allow'd, and breath?
> For death.
>
> ["Another" (II), ll. 1–2]

32. Ibid., p. 135.

From this perspective, one's only hope for avoiding Hell's pain is to mend one's ways, a difficult task for humanity alone.

In contrast, the later meditations on death are much more positive, even cheerful; the reason is that, although the subject is death, the terror of death has now been tamed by meditation on Christ's redemptive sacrifice of himself, which frees the human race from death's power. "On the names Iesus, Christ, Emanuell" focuses on the healing powers of Christ:

> I n vayne we strive to cure our griefe by art,
> E ase, and redresse come only from above,
> S alvation's sent even by the Fathers love
> V nto the sinsicke world, its fester'd heart
> S hall find most ease in balme of Gilead.
> . . . .
> E ach soule repentant he hath Deifi'd;
> M an wholly lost in wickednes, and sinne
> A lone by him, and by his death is freed.
>
> [ll. 1–5, 12–14]

In "On Lazarus rais'd from death," we hear from his own lips Lazarus's story of his cure and resurrection through Christ's intervention told in tones of wonder and gratitude, and in "My last will, and Testament" we hear Colman, confident of God's gifts even to sinsick mortals, dispose of his earthly possessions and concerns. The change of tone evident in these two sequences of meditation on death reflects yet another device of the meditative tradition, the balancing of the depression of self-knowledge against the consoling joy found in knowledge of God's love. In *Audi Filia*, Juan de Avila says,

> They who are much exercised in the *knowledge* of themselves, (in respect that they are continually viewing their defects so neer at hand) are wont to fall into great sadnes, and disconfidence, and pusillanimity; for which reason, it is necessary that they do exercise themselves also in another *knowledge*, which giveth comfort, and strength, much more then the other gave discouragement. . . .
>
> It is therefore fit for thee, after the exercise of the *knowledge of*

thy selfe to imploy thy mind, upon the *knowledge of Christ Iesus our Lord.*[33]

The practice of meditation is, after all, designed to lead one to God, not to suicide, and as St. Bernard knew, self-knowledge and knowledge of God's love are necessary complements. The ultimate thrust of the religious life is positive—toward God, love, creation—and the achievement of this positive goal is the reason St. Bernard gives for seeking self-knowledge.

> Many know many things, & know not themselues: they pry into others, & leaue themselues. They seeke God by those outward things, forsaking their inward things, to which God is neerer, and more inward. Therefore I will returne from outward things, to inward, and from the inward I will ascend to the Superiour: that I may know from whence I come, or whither I goe; who I am, and from whence I am: that so by the knowledge of my selfe, I may be the better able to attaine to the knowledge of God. For by how much more I profit, and goe forward in the knowledge of my selfe, by so much the neerer I approach to the knowledge of God.[34]

It is important to remember that Colman's poems of self-examination are concentrated in the middle section of *Divine Meditations* and are a necessary prelude to the meditations on the Eucharist itself, one of the ways that God reveals Himself to and unites Himself with humanity.

The radical optimism that undergirds *Divine Meditations*, of which we saw evidence in "The Altar" (discussed above, p. 24) is founded on the idea, central to the teachings of both St. Bonaventure and St. Bernard, that the Divine Image in which God created the human race remains, in spite of the Fall, and is capable of being recovered. Our post-lapsarian history sullies and obscures this image but does not destroy it. Through human effort and God's grace, the sinful concretions on the soul can be purged, and the soul, freed from its alienating disguise—now "deiform"

---

33. Juan de Avila, *Audi Filia* ([St. Omer], 1620), pp. 336–38; quoted by Martz, p. 227.
34. *Saint Bernard His Meditations*, pt. 2, pp. 1–2.

in St. Bonaventure's term[35]—can be reunited with God. As Gilson
summarizes St. Bernard's explanation,

> As God made him, he was a noble creature . . . and he was so because
> God created him to His own image. Disfigured by original sin, man
> has in fact exiled himself from the Land of Likeness to enter into the
> Land of Unlikeness: . . . There we have the first inversion of order
> from which all the evil has arisen. . . . Nevertheless, the unlikeness
> has not effaced the image; fear has not annihilated love, servitude to
> sin has not destroyed our natural freedom; in short, the ills we suffer
> by our own fault are not simply substituted for the good things
> that God has heaped upon us, but rather cover them over as with
> another vesture; they hide, but do not eliminate. Underneath this
> hard crust that conceals it, indeformable, indestructible, there still
> subsists the image.[36]

The restlessness, the pain, and the fearfulness of estrangement from God
can be supplanted by the tranquillity, the exuberant health, and the
comfortable trust which follow reunion with the source of one's being
and recovery of one's original identity. It is such a joyful progress, seen in
terms of the Eucharistic liturgy, which shapes Colman's *Divine Meditations*.

HENRY COLMAN'S *DIVINE MEDITATIONS* (1640)

The determining principle of the shape of *Divine Meditations* is the poet's
search for his true identity; only the recovery of his deiform nature can
provide stability, the "rest" denied him by his fallen identity which
condemns him to wander restlessly in exile. Colman projects this idea
through *Divine Meditations* in two magnitudes: first, in the design of the
complete volume, dedicatory material as well as the poetry; and second,
in the order of the poems themselves. In the course of his meditations he

---

35. St. Bonaventura, *The Mind's Road to God*, trans. George Boas (New York, 1953),
chaps. 1, 3, and 4; Etienne Gilson, *The Philosophy of St. Bonaventure*, trans. Dom Illtyd
Trethowan and F. J. Sheed (London, 1938), chap. 14.

36. Gilson, *St. Bernard*, pp. 45, 54.

questions his identity in conjunction with the readings from the Bible prescribed by the lectionary for Lent—readings from the Old Testament which narrate the calling forth and creation of Israel, coupled with the gospel accounts of Christ's passion and resurrection. Colman answers his questions in the form and content of his *Divine Meditations* as he traces his own growth from alienated and intimidated adolescence to confident, competent manhood in terms of the evolution of Israel's relationship with God from her formidable, but rudimentary, encounters as a nomadic tribe with Yahweh under the Old Covenant to the loving companionship of the New Covenant, especially as it is manifested in the Eucharist, the primary sacrament of that covenant.[37]

The dedicatory material is filled with the Old Testament themes that show the beginning of God's revelation of Himself and humanity's first responses to His love. The emphasis is primarily external, focusing on obedience to minutely specific laws concerning outward actions and physical sacrifices of propitiation, rather than on the inward actions and sacrifices of the heart described in "The Altar," the second poem of the volume proper. In the dedicatory letter, Colman portrays himself as a beleaguered wanderer in exile and his patron, William Rokeby, as the source of undeserved, inexplicable grace. He takes the metaphor, of course, from the relationship between the Israelites, particularly Moses, and Yahweh. Rokeby's favors to Colman are "undeserved" and much greater than he can ever repay. Why he has been chosen to receive these blessings is a mystery, but he vows to attempt requital by offering praise, service, and his poems, the *"Primogenitus ingenij"*; he substitutes the first-born of his wit for the firstborn son which was Yahweh's demand from

37. The Covenant parallels and the structure of the Eucharist are apparent in both manuscripts of *Divine Meditations*, for the poems are in the same order, except that the July manuscript has nine additional poems, eight of which Colman inserts at the end of the volume between the double acrostic, "On the Inscription over the head of Christ on the Crosse" (pp. 146–47), and the cruciform poem, "Sinnes Sacrifice" (p. 159). These additional poems can be fitted into the proposed liturgical structure of the volume, but they are, with few exceptions, weaker poems and serve only to dissipate the impetus of the liturgical motion established in the earlier manuscript. Although the substantive changes in the July manuscript are always to the betterment of the individual poem, Colman's concept of the volume as a whole is firmer in the May manuscript. Therefore, the May manuscript, dedicated to William Rokeby, is the basis for the following discussion of *Divine Meditations*.

the Jews. Colman expands the metaphor, even in small details, when he suggests that one reason why his offering of poetry cannot be adequate repayment is that it does not fulfill the requirements for sacrificial oblations stipulated in Leviticus 2:13:

> And every oblation of thy meat offering shalt thou season with salt, neither shalt thou suffer the salt of the covenant of thy God to be lacking from thy meat offering: with all thine offerings thou shalt offer salt.

When Colman offers his poems to Rokeby, he admits regretfully that they "want that salt, that seasoninge" (p. 57) of maturity and asks in "The Invocation" that God supply this lack:

> ... that whatsoe'r I write
> May season'd be by thy diviner Sp'rite.
>
> [ll. 5–6]

Colman reinforces the comparison of Rokeby and Yahweh as "patrons" by emphasizing two definitions of that word: "father-protector" and "pattern to be imitated."[38] It is under Rokeby's protection that Colman's poetry has been written and it is Rokeby's continued protection that will "both stop the mouthes of Calumniators, and illustrate it in despight of any crittical-Detractour." Colman needs Rokeby's help in order to write, for he seems alienated from his companions at the university, much as Moses was in exile in the land of Egypt and needed Yahweh's help to speak to his countrymen. Moses' appeal (Exodus 4:10–12) resembles that of an amateur poet:

> O my Lord, I am not eloquent, neither heretofore, nor since thou hast spoken unto thy servant: but I am slow of speech, and of a slow tongue. And the LORD said unto him, Who hath made man's mouth? or who maketh the dumb, or deaf, or the seeing, or the blind? have not I the LORD? Now therefore go, and I will be with thy mouth, and teach thee what thou shalt say.

---

38. "Pattern" was a doublet of "patron" from the fourteenth to the eighteenth century, and the differentiation was not complete until 1700; see O.E.D., "pattern." In the dedicatory epistle to Savile, Colman plays upon the etymological relation between the two words.

Colman further suggests his lack of assurance as a poet (and therefore his need for protection) by his reference to the "Prologue" of Persius's *Satires*. Colman disclaims, as did Persius, the role of the professional, for whom poetry is the source of money:

> Non fonte labra prolui caballino,
> Nec in bicipiti somniâsse Parnasso
> Memini.

["I never soused my lips in the Nag's Spring (the inspiring spring of Hippocrene, struck out by the hoof of Pegasus, on the top of Mount Helicon); never, that I can remember, did I dream on the two-topped Parnassus." (Loeb Classical Library, *Juvenal and Persius*, English translation by G. G. Ramsey, p. 310)]

Both Persius and Colman are but half-members of the community of bards, somehow chosen to receive the gift of poetic insight from the gods. Persius used his divine inspiration to condemn the excesses of Roman society in his *Satires*; Moses, as messenger for God, indicted the Israelites for their sins against the law and Covenant; and Colman, sharing with both of them the alienation that accompanies special insight, sees himself rejected, and calumny and unjust criticism heaped upon his poetry. Therefore, he both needs and appreciates his patron's protection.

In the second sense of the word *patron*, Rokeby provides a pattern for Colman to imitate, as for example, the early Jews were to pattern their faithfulness to the Covenant on Yahweh's. In Rokeby, Colman finds the "salt and seasoning" of maturity that he himself lacks, and each of the three dedicatory acrostics praises a facet of Rokeby that Colman admires. In the first acrostic, Colman praises the incarnation of goodness (charity) in Rokeby, especially as seen in his charity toward Colman. In the second, Colman praises Rokeby's loyalty to the Anglican church as the orthodox Christian community. In the third, Colman praises Rokeby's submission of his will to God's, a humble obedience that is expressed in the anagrammatizing of his name; Rokeby's name, his ego-identity, is broken apart and reassembled in a slogan—"I broake my will"—that tells of absolute submission to divine will. In his charity, firmness of faith, and complete obedience to God, Rokeby embodies the ideal of Christian life to which Colman, in his youthful confusion, aspires. It is Rokeby's example, as well as his financial assistance, for which Colman is grateful, and he expresses this gratitude by presenting his only wealth, *Divine Meditations*, to his patron.

To see Colman's equation of the relationship between Yahweh and Moses with that between Rokeby and himself as an egregious compliment of poet to patron would be a grave error in the interpretation of tone. Colman is not speaking literally; rather, he is offering a metaphor for the significance of Rokeby's actions in his life, much as Donne pays a literally excessive compliment to Elizabeth Drury in the "Anniversaries," when he portrays the young girl (whom he had never met) as the principle of order in the universe. Colman and Donne transmute Rokeby and Elizabeth Drury from ordinary mortals into symbols of virtue; they become for Colman and Donne examples of those who have succeeded in restoring the Divine Image in themselves and have become thereby the means by which Colman and Donne can perceive God in the fallen world. Rokeby and Elizabeth Drury are never confused in their own or in the poets' minds with God Himself, but always refer the praise of themselves to God, the source of their virtue. As Donne says of Elizabeth Drury at the end of the "Second Anniversary":

> nor would'st thou be content,
> To take this, for my second yeares true Rent,
> Did this Coine beare any other stampe, then his,
> That gave thee power to doe, me, to say this.
> Since his will is, that to posteritie,
> Thou should'st for life, and death, a patterne bee,
> And that the world should notice have of this,
> The purpose, and th'Authoritie is his;
> Thou art the Proclamation; and I am
> The Trumpet, at whose voyce the people came.
>
> [ll. 519–28][39]

39. John Donne, *Poems*, ed. Sir Herbert Grierson (Oxford, 1912), 1:241–42. All further quotations will be taken from this edition.

Elizabeth Drury is the "patterne" of all virtue for Donne:

> Shee whose example they must all implore,
> Who would or doe, or thinke well, and confesse
> That all the vertuous Actions they expresse,
> Are but a new, and worse edition
> Of her some one thought, or one action: ...
> Shee, shee ...
>   is gone
> As well t'enjoy, as get perfection.
> And cals us after her, in that shee tooke,
> (Taking her selfe) our best, and worthiest booke.
> ["The Second Anniversary,"
>   ll. 306–10, 315, 317–20]

Similarly, William Rokeby is the pattern Colman chooses to value and to imitate. For both poets, the imitation of their patterns is the imitation of Christ at one remove.

In opposition to this dedicatory matter with its unmistakable Old Testament themes, Colman sets the poems of *Divine Meditations*. In his letter to Rokeby, he called it the "remedie for my disturbed mind," and the order of the poems in the volume discloses the means of his cure. This "remedie" is found in the controlling image of *Divine Meditations*, the church's liturgy of the Eucharist. The liturgy is singularly appropriate for the description of the journey from exile to the ultimate companionship of the heavenly banquet and divine presence, for that journey is recapitulated in the form of the liturgy, which begins with the psalms and the lessons of the Old Testament,[40] shows the fulfillment of prophecy by the Incarnation as preached in the Epistles and described in the Gospels, and culminates in the active participation of each person in the redemptive fellowship of the Eucharistic meal, when he takes Christ's body into his own in the form of the bread and wine. From this communal action of the church, Colman derives his strength and his identity, for at the table

---

40. The psalms and the lessons from the Old Testament are not part of the liturgy itself but come from the lections appointed for the daily office that customarily precedes the liturgy.

of the Eucharist, the wanderer finds his true home, the sick is restored to health, and love—not detraction or calumny—rules. The speaker of the dedication defined himself in terms of the Old Covenant, but the speaker of the poems embodies the knowledge of the New Covenant that the church celebrates in the Eucharist. Colman's plan for his book is to mirror the complementary relationship between Old and New Covenants in the contrast between his dedication and the volume of poetry itself, and the reason why he chooses the Eucharist as the organizing principle for his book is that the Eucharist has been the manifestation of the New Covenant from the first days after the Resurrection throughout time.

The poems of *Divine Meditations* are grouped in distinct sequences that correspond to the main sections of the Eucharistic ritual. The first sequence of meditations resembles the instructional part of the Eucharist, the *synaxis*, which derives from Jewish synagogue worship and consists of invocations, psalms, and the reading of the Scriptures; the second part of the liturgy is the actual celebration of the Eucharist meal, the consecration and distribution of the bread and wine.[41] Between and in addition to these two main parts of the liturgy, Colman inserts the series of poems of self-examination and self-judgment, of personal preparation for receiving the Sacrament. He is fully justified by church practice, for after the reading of the propers for the day, the priest frequently read the Exhortation to those who remained and planned to make their communions; he said, echoing St. Paul (1 Corinthians 11:28–29):

> my duty is to exhort you to consider the dignity of the holy mysterie, and the great peril of unworthy receiving thereof, and so to search and examine your own consciences, as ye may come holy and clean to a most godly and heavenly feast, so that in no wise you come but in the marriage-garment required of God in holy scripture, and so come, and be received, as worthy partakers of such a heavenly table. The way and means thereto, is; First, to examine your lives and conversation.[42]

41. Dom Gregory Dix, *The Shape of the Liturgy* (London, 1964), chaps. 1–5, especially chap. 3.

42. *The Book of Common Prayer, and Administration of the Sacraments: and other rites and ceremonies of the Church of England: With the Psalter, or Psalmes of David* (Cambridge, 1638), sig. C₅v.

Colman thus constructs his volume of poetry on the liturgical pattern of the Eucharist: first, the meditations on biblical texts that reflect the lectionary for Lent and Eastertide (perhaps the spring that preceded his gift of his poems to Rokeby and Savile); second, a preparation of the soul for the Eucharist by self-examination and meditations on his sins and the means of redemption; and third, meditations on the Eucharist itself, in which he examined its meaning, source, and effects. In the shape of the liturgy and, consequently, *Divine Meditations*, we can see the movement toward self-knowledge and reunion with God that St. Bernard vowed:

> Therefore I will returne from outward things, to inward, and from the inward I will ascend to the Superiour: that I may know from whence I come, or whither I goe; who I am.

The objective knowledge of God's love that Colman gains through the lections of the *synaxis*, he later takes within himself and applies to his own particular needs as preparation for the ascent "to the Superiour." This encounter with the "Superiour" is, in terms of the Eucharist, the ingestion of the elements of bread and wine, representing Christ's body and blood.

The meditations of the first segment—from "The Altar" through "On the Spirit adulterated by the flesh"—draw their subjects from the lections appointed for Lent and imitate the order of the *synaxis*. "The Altar," among its other functions in the design of the volume, recalls the beginning of the service itself, for it paraphrases the prefatory sentence for matins during Lent, "The sacrifices of God are a broken spirit: a broken and contrite heart, O God, thou wilt not despise" (Psalm 51:17). The next two poems, "On God's Mercie" and "On my enemies vniust malice," are meditations on typical psalm-themes: praise for God's goodness and complaint under affliction by pagans. In the remainder of poems in the first section, Colman emphasizes the traditional Lenten pairing of the story of the creation of Israel (the Old Covenant) with the story of God's redemption of mankind (the New Covenant). First, we find a meditation, consisting of three poems, on mortality and immortality based on a text from Genesis. The text (Genesis 47:9) is Jacob's estimate of his life when, in old age, he is saved from famine by his long-lost son Joseph, who is a type of Jesus as Savior. Jacob reflects on his past life and acknowledges his sinfulness. The second poem in this sequence has the ring of prophetic indictment; a righteous voice points out the sins of the materialistic, back-sliding "chosen people." The third poem ends the Old Testament meditation with a joyous injunction to seek immortality, for heavenly joys are far greater than earthly ones. The next five poems meditate the accounts of the Passion in the Gospel lections for Holy Week, and "On the Spirit adulterated by the flesh" concludes these meditations with Colman's contemplation of the relation of the spirit to the flesh in himself and his finding himself far short of Jesus' example. This realization of his own sinfulness ends the meditations of the *synaxis* and turns Colman's mind to self-examination and preparation for receiving the sacrament.

The second part of *Divine Meditations* represents the time of preparation for receiving the Eucharist. In this part of Colman's book, we find the alternation between knowledge of self, which often brings sadness, and knowledge of God's love, which brings comfort and encouragement, that Juan de Avila recommended in *Audi Filia* (see above, p. 30). Colman shows the meditating mind moving in cycles from contemplation of sins to the means of redemption, but after each meditation on redemption, the poet's mind returns to the problems of living in a fallen world. Each return to earthly considerations seems a failure to attain permanent comfort, but there is a kind of progress in the poet's deepening perception of the means of salvation. The three cycles of preparation are marked by ever more immediate realizations of the divine presence. First, the poet merely aspires to praise God by prayer ["On Prayer" (p. 97), "Another" (p. 98)]; then he perceives Christ as the healer of his sinsickness ["On the names Iesus, Christ, Emanuell" (p. 109)]; finally, he meditates on the Incarnation, the transcendence of the separation of the height of Heaven from the lowness of earth ["On the life of Christ" (p. 123), "On his Birth. A Pastorall" (p. 125), "On his Birth-day" (p. 127)]. After these cycles of preparation, the poet is ready to receive the Eucharist, the meal by which he is nourished and strengthened for his continuing attempt to imitate Christ in the present.

The middle section of *Divine Meditations* begins with explicit self-examination (see the "Judgment" sequence, pp. 88–96). This action is

meticulous preparation for receiving the Eucharist, and the poems re-
sound with overtones of the Final Judgment, for the Eucharist is the
earthly type of the ultimate feast of the faithful in Heaven (Revelation 19).
After the Judgment sequence come two poems "On Prayer." In the first,
the poet acknowledges his sin and expresses his desire to pray, even
though he has only sighs and groans to offer to God. In the second poem,
prayer is defined as the "way to health" for those who are sick, and thus
this poem anticipates the predominant theme of the second cycle, death
and sickness. The meditator is just beginning his journey to God and
prays for grace to continue it:

> Grante me grace then Lord that I
> May with fervent prayer crie
> To thy goodnes, and ne'r cease
> Till from thee I've purchas'd peace.
>
> [ll. 21–24]

Thus ends the first cycle of preparation.

In the second cycle, the poet returns to self-examination, this time by
seeing his life from the perspective of death. After three poems about
death, he considers various sins or pitfalls that can lead one to eternal
death, beginning, appropriately enough, with drunkenness, which causes
the death of human reason and the consequent release of bestiality. Other
pitfalls are physical desire (to be controlled by marriage), the allure of
outward beauty, and anger. After his admission of his tendency toward
these sins, the poet meditates on the remedy for them: "On the names
Iesus, Christ, Emanuell." As an example of God's healing power, the poet
meditates "On Lazarus, rais'd from death"; Lazarus's desire to be prepared
and fit in soul to meet his "reck'ninge day" stirs Colman to make his
"last will and Testament," for, as the concluding poem of this cycle ("On
Time") tells, all things die, even time itself. Therefore, the soul must
prepare for eternity, and that preparation demands a righteous life on earth:

> For who the death o'th'righteous would die
> On earth must labour to live righteouslie.
>
> [ll. 39–40]

Here the third cycle begins, as the mind of the poet comes back to earth and to the problems of living a righteous life in a world of deceptive appearances. The first poem of this cycle, "On Deformitie," defines this problem as the lack of correlation between interior reality and exterior appearance:

> The fairest face oft owes the foulest heart,
>   And doth (though goodnes showe)
>   Noe virtue owe,
> And often though deform'd i'th'outward parte
>   A heart we find
> Season'd with grace, and heavenly goodnes soe
>   As showes a mind
> Where noe deformitie, or vice doth growe.
>
> [ll. 13–20]

The next poem, "On Pride," traces the source of this chaos to the basic sin, or deformity, of the world, pride—that by which we turn from worshiping God to worshiping ourselves. By this action, the original harmony of life is shattered into discordant fragments, the "hateful seige of contraries" (to borrow Milton's phrase) that so tormented Lucifer. Only by reconciling the opposing "contraries" of appearance and reality can the deceptiveness of the earthly life be eliminated, and the poet begins such a reconciliation in the last stanza of this meditation by redefining pride:

> But if we must be proud of ought, graunt Lord
> We may reioyce in thy most holy word.
>   Let our pride, and glory be
>   Of noe vaine, noe worldly thinge,
>   But let vs exult in thee
>   And thy crosse eternall Kinge,
>   Let vs suffer all disgrace
>   Proudly, that the world can lay,
>   And all sufferings imbrace
>   For thy sake, we humbly pray,

> Let our pride, and glory be
> In thy crosse alone, and thee.
> Thus to be proud is glory, not a fault,
> This pride shall God himselfe to heaven exalt.
>
> [ll. 57–70]

In "On Humilitie," the poet finds humility to be identical with pride as he has just redefined it. Humility is apparently of the earth (from L. *humus*)

> yet its branch aspires
> High as the greate Iehovah's sacred quires,
> And thither tends from whence it first tooke birth.
>
> [ll. 2–4]

Humility transcends all earthly distinctions and gives to mortals all the power and majesty they could desire; in fact, humility is the only way to achieve the godhead that Lucifer sought and lost through pride:

> Profitt, and pleasure both this Angell [humility] brings,
> Better then can the purest angell-gold
> This, (more then all his miracles) hath told
> The world, our Saviour Christ's the King of Kings.
> 'Tis this that makes men Angells, more then soe
> Like God, yea gods themselves, by this alone
> Th'are made Christ's partners i'th'eternall throne.
>
> [ll. 31–37]

In these two poems, Colman reconciles the "contraries" of pride and humility through meditation.

The ultimate reconciliation of the earthly shards of divine order—the apparent "contraries" of high and low, pride and humility, fairness and foulness—is found in the following meditations about Christ that are the culmination of the third cycle of preparation. In "On the life of Christ," the story of Christ's life allegorized as that of a black swan, the elemental fairness does become "foul" in the Incarnation, as the divine and the human are joined together. "On his Birth. A Pastorall" is a dramatization of the Nativity that focuses on the proud Magi and the humble shepherds who are united in, and because of, their mutual search for the Christ Child. The Magi must ask the shepherds' help, and they join them in songs of praise, as Christ the Black Swan taught in the previous poem. But the next Christmas meditation, "On his Birth-day," turns from this vision of the ideal unity back to the realities of earthly life; the tone of this poem is somber, for meditation on the Incarnation inevitably entails thoughts of the Crucifixion: Christ was born as a man so that he might atone for human sinfulness with his death.

The two poems which follow the meditations on the Incarnation, "On ioy" and "On Mourning," are a transition between the highest peak of perception about redemption and the redemptive meal itself. In these two poems, the mood plummets from joy at the contemplation of Jesus himself to crabbed pessimism and *contemptus mundi*. Earthly joy is a counter-feit and should be despised; mourning is the way of life by which one soonest comes to a truly joyful afterlife in heaven. It is as if by knowing the scope of God's mercy, the poet becomes painfully aware of the scope of his own unworthiness. While oppressed by the sense of his own desolation, Colman receives "The Invitation" and begins his meditations on the Eucharist—the remedy and the redemption for all, even for himself.

"The Invitation" offers to rich and poor, diseased and sound, beggar and king—every one a "sinfull wight" (line 1)—a seat at the Holy Table and the opportunity to partake of Christ Himself. As the cycles of prep-aration were aimed both at the receiving of the Eucharist and at the gaining of eternal life in Heaven (cf. the Judgment sequence, the many references to the crown of eternal life in the other poems of preparation), so "The Invitation" is both to the Eucharist (ll. 13–18) and to the Feast of the Lamb of Revelation 19 (line 2). The only requirement for either meal is contrition and repentance, and "The Invitation" draws together many of the themes of self-examination found in the middle section of the volume and focuses them on the meal itself. "On the Lords Supper" begins in a freful key:

> Foule I am and cannot tell
> How to purge me,

Sad I am yet dare not showe
        What doth vrge me,
Sicke I am, and would be well
        But doe not knowe
What member is most payned,
        Distress'd I am
        'Bove any man
Yet cannot tell where comfort might be gayned.

[ll. 1–10]

In the second stanza, however, calm assurances quiet each one of the speaker's complaints:

Christ's bloud is the sacred oyle
        To make thee white,
By his bloud (though ne'r soe sad)
        Thou may'st be light,
            And glad;
Hee's a salve can make thee smile
        Though ne'r soe bad,
And will soone thy sicknes cure,
        He thy distresse
        Will sure make lesse,
And he alone can comfort best assure.

[ll. 11–21]

The rest of the poem is calm, confident explanation of the redemption and the Eucharist, the sign of the New Covenant between God and His people. From this point in the volume to its conclusion, the poems show security and self-confidence absent before. Within each step of the first two segments, a tension between the promises of God and the ways of the world gnawed at Colman (see, for example, the psalm-poems "On Gods mercie" and "On my enemies vniust malice"). Within the Eucharist, the gap between intellectual and experiential knowledge has been closed.

Other poems in this final segment of the book are meditations on subjects closely related to the Eucharist. "To the Church" praises the

institution which is the means of the distribution of the Eucharist, and
"A vowe" is the poet's plan for showing his gratitude for God's grace.
Both poems show that all of the speaker's agony is past, and he has been
purged and unified with Christ. In contrast to these two poems, the night-
mare of "A Dreame" is a shock, but its horror is a measure of the poet's
gratitude for the Eucharist; the memory of his former torments, intruding
on his recently attained health, throws the past into ghastly perspective.
"On Christ's wounded side, and the soldier" is a meditation on the source
of the sacraments of Baptism and the Eucharist, the wounding of Jesus'
side from which flowed water and blood; the poet sees this cowardly
deed as a *felix culpa*, for by it the wounded one is able to heal the inflicter
of the wound. The next poems, "On Povertie" and "On Affliction,"
themselves have little to do with the Eucharist, but they certainly exemplify
the health to which the poet has been restored in the course of the liturgy.
In the first, the poet vows to incarnate in himself Christ's charity, and in
"On Affliction" he perceives the reason for his afflictions and can explain
without fear that

> Affliction is a sure, and certaine signe
>   Of Gods exceedinge love,
>   'Tis the divine
>   Expression of his care
>   By which he strives to move
> His from their follies, and would teach them come
>   With reverent feare
> And hearty penitence to heaven their home.
>   O bless'd affliction that do'st winne
> Sinners, 'tis good they have afflicted beene.

[ll. 11–20]

The figure of the incarnate Christ is the focal point of the last two
poems. In "On the Inscription over the head of Christ on the Crosse,"
Colman meditates with unrelenting persistence on the most poignant
consequence of the Incarnation, the Crucifixion; he sees and hears both
the power and the pain, the love and the regal ire of Jesus, as He suffers the

full burden of fallen human nature. Jesus urges sinners to turn away from
the world toward Him:

>   O let it pittie then move in you soe
>   As may constraine you to repentance g O
>   F   erret remorse, and that inioyne you doffe
>   Sinnes damned garment, and all vice put of F.
>
>   [ll. 6a–7b]

Then, seeing the spectacle of the Crucifixion, they may become "Knit,
and ingrafted into me" (line 19a) so that, by his suffering and their proper
appreciation of it,

>   though now I weep E
>   S   orrow shall be exil'd, and I noe lesse
>   Happie in death, then you in happine S.
>
>   [ll. 31b–32b]

The name that shapes the poem ("Iesus of Nazareth, the King of the
Iewes") is the earthly identity that has brought Jesus such suffering; but
this suffering is also the place of the reunion of fallen humanity with God.
This union is fully evident in the final poem of *Divine Meditations*, "Sinnes
Sacrifice."

"Sinnes Sacrifice" is the culmination of Colman's book for several
reasons. First, Colman molds the poem into the shape of the cross and
links himself with both the suffering and the triumph of Christ. The poem
is a vow to imitate Christ, for Colman's awareness of Christ's redemption
of the human race impels him from the realm of pure devotion toward
righteous action, as he vows to incarnate in his life the extent of love shown
by Christ. Second, the very shape of the poem crystallizes the contrast
between Old and New Covenants, for it is one of the two "shaped" poems
of *Divine Meditations*, the other being "The Altar."

Both poems, altar-shaped and cruciform, are placed significantly in the
volume. The clay altar is placed at the beginning of the volume, for the
sacrifices of the clay altar were incomplete, offered, as they were, in only
partial knowledge of God's love; this shape suggests the poet's ignorance

of his identity as he began his meditations. The emphasis on the Old Covenant in that poem's shape reinforces the persona Colman develops in the dedicatory introduction to the book. Found at the end of the volume, the cross, the emblem of the complete sacrifice of the New Covenant, suggests that, at this final point in his meditations, the poet has achieved an understanding of who he is, and this suggestion is reflected in the health and fearlessness of his spirit in the last meditations—fearlessness which St. Bernard calls *fiducia*, the sure sign of the presence of God within the soul. As Gilson explains *fiducia*, "the progress of love consists in the passage from a state in which a man is a slave to fear . . . to another in which he purely and simply loves. For love banishes fear."[43] The biblical text for St. Bernard is St. John's treatise on the love of God, the First Epistle:

> Herein is our love made perfect, that we may have boldness in the day of judgment: because as he is, so are we in this world. There is no fear in love; but perfect love casteth out fear: because fear hath torment. He that feareth is not made perfect in love.

> [1 John 4:17–18]

Thus, the beginning and the end of the volume are marked by the emblems of the Covenants—sacrificial altar of propitiatory offerings and the cross of Christ's redemptive oblation of himself—and Colman has used the Eucharistic liturgy as the formal pattern of his book, tracing the path to self-knowledge from outward instruction through purgatorial self-examination to final union with God in the sacrament.

Divine Meditations, in yet another way, represents a progress toward the Divine as the essence of order, and in this progress Colman unites his vocation as a Christian with his vocation as a poet. From the first, Colman shows a strong desire for order. Indeed, the epigraph for *Divine Meditations* testifies to this desire: *Studiosus diem dividit, Otiosus frangit* ("The zealous student apportions the day; the idle man shatters it in pieces.") In his letter to William Rokeby, he explains that, rather than submit to the conclusions of his meditations, make up the book that, in substance

---

43. Gilson, *St. Bernard*, p. 24.

find noe better remedie" than meditation, the conclusions of which he "digested into writinge ... [and] shape"—and formed into the poems of this volume. He uses meditation as a way of ordering the events of his life into a comprehensible pattern, lest he become merely a passive victim of random occurrences.

"Sinnes Sacrifice," Colman's final meditation, illuminates a way to understand why writing this book was a "remedie" for Colman's distress. The meaning of the title—literally, the "making holy of sin"—is clarified in the first lines of the poem, which tell how evil things can be turned into good if they are transformed from their natural state—in which one has little understanding of them and no mastery over them—into "artifacts"— things that whoever has made can voluntarily "lift up" as an offertory to God.

> Behold the Lambe-of-God lift vp on high,
> Of whom the brazen serpent was a type,
> That look'd on heal'd, and was a remedie
> Against the stinginge serpents poyson'd bite.
>
> [ll. 1–4]

Colman's two images come from the Old and the New Testaments. When poisonous serpents were killing the Israelites, God ordered Moses, "Make thee a fiery serpent, and set it upon a pole: and it shall come to pass, that every one that is bitten, when he looketh upon it, shall live" (Numbers 21:8); Moses made the serpent of brass and it removed the power of death from the natural serpents. The Gospel of John (3:14) links this incident with the Crucifixion: "And as Moses lifted up the serpent in the wilderness, even so must the Son of man be lifted up." Because Christ made the offering of Himself to be "lifted up" on the cross (in appearance, the same death that criminals were forced to endure), his death, like the "brazen serpent," took away the power of death over man.

Colman transcends the confusion and evil in his own life in this same way. His "remedie" for the enemies, the temptations, the ridicule, and the persecution is to master them by meditation and to make them, as poems, into the sign of his victory. His poems, polished from the "rough-cast" conclusions of his meditations, make up the book that, in substance

and shape, proclaims his recovery of the Divine Image in which he was created and his triumph over the sinful world.

In conclusion, *Divine Meditations* is a welcome addition to the canon of seventeenth-century religious poetry. It is valuable evidence for the scholar, and much more besides. Although the quality of the poems ranges from excellent to mediocre, there are some that flash with the wit of Donne or sing with the complex harmony of Herbert. To appreciate Colman's special gifts, however, the volume should be read as a whole, for then one can clearly see the action of a vigorous mind that refuses to accept chaos as the basic principle of life, and in this refusal asserts both its humanity and its divinity.

Divine Meditations

DIVINE
MEDITATI-
-ONS.

By
H: C: Philo-musus.

Studiosus diem dividit, Otiosus frangit.

Maij xx°:
1640.

To the Worshipfull my honour'd Kinsman, and most approved freind William Rokeby Esquire.

Sir

Having languished (as your selfe partly knowes) vnder many late afflictions, and especially that of miserable necessity, I could find noe better remedie for my disturbed mind, then to evade calamities by Meditation; and at my Horae successivæ falling into many considerations, I now, and then digested some of them into writinge, even in the shape (except a little more rough-cast) that I now present them you, and had thought (scribling them over in loose papers) never to have reveal'd them further then my private recreation, but considering at last that I stood ingag'd to you, in a strickt tie for your (vndeserved) favours, and fearinge least I might never be better able to make requitall otherwise, collectinge my papers wch before lay neglectedly scattered, and willing to shew the zeale I have, both to expresse my gratitude, and doe you service, I was emboldened to make a tender of my respects to you by this *Primogenitus ingenij,* which my humble request is, you will mercifully deigne to shelter vnder your gracious patronage, beinge assured that however weake, and invaluable in it selfe, yet your goodnes will both stop the mouthes of Calumniators, and illustrate it, in despight of any critticall-Detractour: I confesse I may well with *Persius* the Satyrist crie out with admiration

Non fonte labra prolui caballino,
Nec in bicipiti somniâsse Parnasso
Memini.

And therefore how I am become a Dabbler in the *Muses* incke this is the thinge, the wonder; Indeed I know these *Meditations* want that salt, that seasoninge, that might befitt either a learned writer, or a Iuditious Supervisor, yet such as they are receiue them, as the offering of a heart who with all thankfullnesse

Presents it selfe Your
vnfeigned servant

Henry Colman
And Dedicates to your
vnparralell'd virtue
his
Divine
Meditations.

Anacrostica Dedicatoria. [I]

V irtue alone enobles, to be greate,
V vise, wealthy, or what'ever may be more,
I s to be nothing if with vice repleate,
L earning, when ioyn'd with sacred wisedomes lore
L eads the possessors to a glorious seate,   5
I n you, these ample are, and to the poore
A llwaies have beene assistant, I haue felt
M uch charity hath in your bosome dwelt.

R elligion doth inioyne vs gratitude
O bediently be paid to whom 'tis due,   10
K indnesse commands from me a multitude
E ven to my full power I pay to you,
B lesse but my labour with acceptance then,
Y ou haue more then made me vp a man agen.

Anacrostica Dedicatoria. [II]

W hat is our life but sorrow, can we find
I n this fraile world, ought but a troubled mind?
L earning's depraved, and the sacred Writ
L ewdly perverted is, and ev'ry wit
I n selfe-opinion strikes vpon that way   5
A lone, that leads to ruine, most doe stray
M uch from the sincere truth, soe vaine's our clay.

R elligion's made a mocke: soe that to know
O ne truely greate, and good now, is to show
K nowledge a miracle, and I confesse   10
E nough in you these shine, Virtue doth blesse
'B ove Wealth your life, and I will ever pray
Y our after may be crown'd, this life be gray.

Anacrostica Dedicatoria. [III]

Ἀναγρᾰμμα.

I broake my will.

Epigr.

W ealth many doe enioy, but where to find
(I n one and the same subiect,) out a mind
L abours to master wealth, and breake his will
(L east loving it, or any baser ill,
I t might betray him to a fond desire,   5
A nd make him slave to sinne) this doth require
M ore then a common man, an earthly fire.

R arely your nature in your name's express'd
O nly anagrammatiz'd, your nature bless'd:
K nowledge hath taught, and show'd you conquer ill,   10
E xpress'd in this resolve I broake my will;
B est is that Valour, choicest Victory
Y ields conquest o'r th'affections tyrannie.

Anacrostica Dedicatoria. [IV]

H aving noe wealth to shew my gratitude
E xcept this of my Braine, how'ever crude;
N or willing to be held ingratefull where
R eceiu'd ingagements doe commaund me beare
Y ou much respect, I held it not amisse   5

C loth'd as it is (Sir) to present you this:
O nly my hope is, (though vnlearn'd, vndress'd)
L oue will soe shadow o'r what's weake express'd
M y zeale shall not be slighted, but will find
A courteous censure, soe (Sir) shall you bind   10
N ature, as name to honour your brave mind.

Philo-poëticus.

DIVINE
MEDITATI-
-ONS.

By H: C: Philo-poeticus.

Studiosus diem diuidit, Otiosus frangit

Secundo Iulij
Anno
1640

To the right Worshipfull Sir William Savile Baronett Patron of Arts, and Armes, and true Patterne of noble piëtie, and virtue.

Right worshipfull

Your virtue (like the Loadstone) attracts both the love, and admiration of all that eyther knowe, or have truely heard of you, and I doubt not but your temporall greatnes heere, will instruct you labour greatnes to eternitie. I confesse my selfe one of those farthest from your knowledge, yet know my selfe (and desire to be knowne) neere you in my respect; and therefore have, (as an humble earnest of my future zeale to your vnimitable virtue) thus boldly tendered you, this humble *Primogenitus* of my infant Muse, not knowinge (indeed) to whom I might more fitly present it, then to your worthy selfe, which howsoever I confesse it wants that *Salem Ingenij*, and smells not of the Lampe like the industrious labours of sublimer fancies, yet cannot it choose but flourish vnder the Protection of soe apparent goodnes: Accept it Sir I beseech you as the offeringe of an humble heart, who if it should meete with a denyall might strangle its Muse in the Cradle, but receiv'd, and cherish'd vp, vnder your noble flame, you shall obliege in all the faculties of a gratefull mind

> The humblest of your Servants
> Henry Colman.
> who at your feete submissively
> layes
>> his
>> Divine Meditations.

Anacrostica.

S uch, and soe vitious is this age that where
I n greatnesse goodnesse chiefest sway doth beare
R enders the man miraculous and rare.

W hat is it lesse in you, who are noe lesse
I n virtue greate, then rich in happinesse,   5
L earning, and Armes share equally your breast,
L oyaltie in your Princes favour makes you blessed.
I t is your glory you were thought to be
A man for wisedome, and for pietie
M ost fit to ioyne, your Shiere to rectifie   10

S hould they have sought a man in all compleate,
A s fitt as they could wish for such a feate,
(V nlesse yourselfe) they might haue sought about
I n every angle of the Shiere throughout,
L abour'd in vaine, but when they found out you   15
E xactly did you make their iudgments true.

B less'd may you ever be, and may you liue
A lway as happie as this life can give
R enown'd may you be heere, and may you growe
O ld, and much honour may your old age knowe;   20
N o sad misfortune crosse your happinesse
E xcept to better you, may Angells blesse
T il death your life, and may you live to be
T enfold more happie in Eternitie.

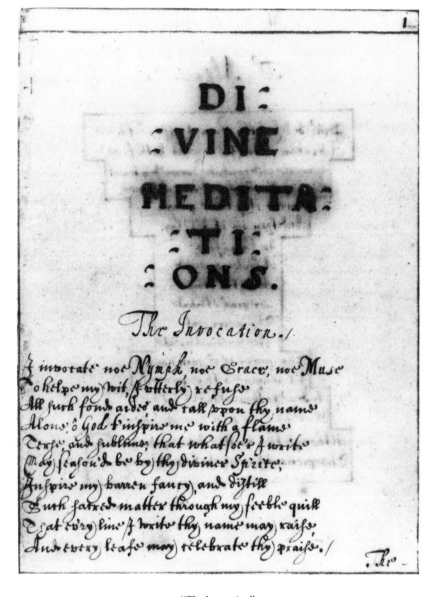

DIVINE MEDITATIONS.

The Invocation. 1

I invocate noe Nymph, noe Grace, noe Muse
To helpe my wit, I vtterly refuse
All such fond aides, and call vpon thy name
Alone ô God t'inspire me with a flame
Terse and sublime: that whatsoe'r I write
May season'd be by thy divine Spirite;
Inspire my barren fancy, and distill
Such sacred matter through my feeble quill
That every line I write thy name may raise,
And every leafe may celebrate thy praise.

DI-
-VINE
MEDITA-
-TI-
-ONS.

The Invocation.

I invocate noe Nymph, noe Grace, noe Muse
To helpe my wit, I vtterly refuse
All such fond aides, and call vpon thy name
Alone, ô God t'inspire me with a flame
Terse, and sublime; that whatsoe'r I write   5
May season'd be by thy diviner Sp'rite;
Inspire my barren fancy, and distill
Such sacred matter through my feeble quill
That ev'ry line I write thy name may raise,
And every leafe may celebrate thy praise.   10

Behold (o Lord) thy Servant offers thee
A broken Altar, 'tis a heart both free
Humble, and contrite, drown'd in teares
(High swollen w:th sighes, w:th sobbs, w:th teares)
Accept it I thee pray,
And then on it I'll lay
In sacrifice ∞∞
A soule renew'd,
And still devise
By prayse 'tentrude
Thy mercy: Sate
How wondrous great
∞ || ∞ || ∞ || ∞ || ∞
∞ || ∞ || ∞ || ∞ || ∞
Thy goodnes is, each houre
I'll magnifie thy power
And as to thee alone, I offer
Soe, I beseech thee doe not suffer;
Although the brittle Altar passe to clay,
The pretious intruse to be cast away.

D2

"The Altar"
Rawlinson poetical manuscript 204
The Bodleian Library

The Altar.

Behold ô Lord thy servant offers thee
A broken Altar, 'tis a heart both free
    Humble, and contrite, drown'd in teares
    High swoll'n with sighes, with sobbes, with feares.
        Accept it I thee pray,   5
        And then on it I'l lay
            In sacrifice
            A soule renew'd,
            And still devise
            By pray'r t'intrude   10
            Thy mercy seate
            For wondrous greate
        Thy goodnes is, each houre
        I'l magnifie thy power,
    And as to thee alone I offer,   15
    Soe (I beseech thee) doe not suffer,
Although the brittle Altar passe to Clay,
The precious Incense to be cast away.

On God's Mercie.

How good a God thou art, how greate, and free
     Thy mercies are to mee,!
Yea, though each moment I my sinnes renew
     And soe become Hells due,
Yet thou in mercy pluck'st me from the brincke   5
     And wilt not let me sincke;
All thy Corrections doe in mercy fall,
Teach my poore heart to give thee thankes for all.

Thou art the Potter (Lord) and I the Clay,
     By thee alone I stay,   10
If thou have fram'd me for dishonour, shall
     I dare repine at all?
If thou correct me for my sinnes, ô God,
     I'l kneele, and kisse the rod;
For thy afflictions are but mercy still,   15
Teach my hard heart obedience to thy will.

I am thy creature, vse thy pleasure (Lord,)
     Renew me by thy word,
O circumcise the foreskin of my heart,
     Let it in every part   20
Be soft, and tender flesh: honour my soule
     In thy eternall rowle,
I begge noe more; then happie I will singe
Perpetuall prayse, to thee th'Almighty Kinge.

On my enemies vniust malice.

Loden with cares, oppress'd with woe,
Mine enemies encompasse me,
And strive thy servant downe to throwe
Because I put my trust in thee,
But thou that do'st their malice see   5
Shalt venge, and answeare Lord for me.

Their tongues sharpe swords, and arrowes are,
With which they warre against my life,
Their words more sharpe, and bitter farre,
Would faine provoke to wicked strife,   10
But thou that do'st their malice see
Shalt venge, and answeare Lord for me.

Be I abroad, they straightway crie
Hee's to some vicious service gone,
And dogge me at the heeles, to spie   15
What greate offences I have done;
But thou that do'st their malice see
Shalt venge, and answeare Lord for mee.

Stay I at home, they then exclame;
Be with them, and their scornes expresse   20
Their desp'rate hate, and to their shame
My absence malice they noe lesse.
But thou that do'st their malice see
Shalt venge, and answeare Lord for me.

Goe I to Church, or pray at home,   25
Sollicitinge thy goodnes there,
To grante me wisedome, that alone
I thee may reverence, and feare;
They crie, marke his hypocrisie,
But thou shalt answeare Lord for me.   30

If I be poore they me despise,
If I a competency have,
Th'are wicked goods they straight surmise,
And desp'rately against me rave,
To ruine me they all agree,   35
But thou shalt answeare Lord for me.

If thou art pleas'd my life to blesse,
They mutter, and with envy pine,
But if thou make my prosper lesse,
Lord how they ioy at my decline;   40
Thou know'st, and seest how ill they bee,
Revenge, and answeare Lord for me.

And thus with care oppress'd, with woe
On ev'ry side incompass'd round,
Didd'st not thou keepe me Lord, I know   45
I suddenly should fall to ground;
But thou that do'st their malice se
Shalt venge and answeare Lord for me.

On Mortalitie.

Few, & evill have the dayes of the yeares of my life been—Gen: 47:9

The world's deceitfull, and mans life at best
　　　Is but a life vndress'd,
　　　　　And voyd of rest,
　Scarce a span-longe, fraile as the brittlest glasse,
　　　And like the wither'd grasse   5
　　　　　It hence doth passe;
　Who trusts the world then, or man's brittle fate,
　Reckons without his host, betrayes his state.

Each bubble (fitly) represents to man
　　　His life, and (broken) can   10
　　　　　Shew him his span,
　Soe vayne, and fraile's the greatest mortalls stay,
　　　That ev'ry moment may
　　　　　His life betray;
　Grante then ô Lord that I may trust in none,   15
　Neyther the world, nor man, but thee alone.

Noe sooner are we borne into the light,
　　　But presently we fright,
　　　　　And bid good night,
　As if our birth-day were but giv'n to spie   20
　　　The world, and at it crie,
　　　　　And straightway die,
　Thus assoone dead, as borne, assoone forgot,
　Scarce any knowinge that we were or not.

If God doe please to lengthen out our dayes,   25
　　　And give vs tyme to raise
　　　　　His name, and praise;
　Our longest time is but an hundred yeares,
　　　And those soe full of feares,
　　　　　Soe mix'd with cares   30

That never any soe long-liv'd was seene,
But all his dayes have few, and evill beene.

Our infancie is altogether crosse,
    Our childish-age but losse,
        Our youth meere drosse,   35
Once growne vp to be men, we then presume
    We may our lives consume
        In drincke, and fume,
And our old age (meere dotage) is the worst;
Soe each scene fills vp but a life accurss'd.   40

If while we live heere we doe health enioy,
    Honour, or wealth vs cloy
        And make vs coy,
If we have all delights the world can give,
    Yet we shall wretched live   45
        Only to grieve;
For the world's pompe, and earth's felicitie,
Is only constant in vnconstancie.

Shall I then doate, and be in love with earth,
    Or any mortall birth?   50
        Or feare a death
That I must pay? O rather let me strive
    (While I am heere alive)
        Only to give
My life to thee; and grante that when I die   55
Lord, I may reigne with thee eternallie.

Another.

Wretched mortalls why are you
Soe in love with bubble-breath?
Since your dayes are ill, and few
Every way besett with death?

Tell me, thou that hoord'st vp gold   5
And do'st love vngodly wealth,
Can for an hundred Fifty-fold,
Bringe thy sinfull soule its health?

Tell me drunckard do'st thou thinke
That thy life will ever last,   10
To be spent in fume and drinke
That thou spend'st it soe in wast?

Glutton leave to fill thy mawe,
With the daintyest-costly fare,
And let youth be kept in awe,   15
And all fornication feare.

Thinke not lick'rish Lady none
Sees thy beastly wanton-lust,
All thy whorish acts are knowne
To the Father of the iust.   20

Paint, and curle, crispe, and perfume,
Disguise you in what antique dresse
You'l devise, yet thus presume
Death will know you ne'rthelesse.

Thinks the Mimicke to disguise   25
Him, from Time's devouringe hand,?
Or the forsworne tradesmans lies
That death cannot vnderstand?

Yes, let mortalls (fondlings) knowe

That their ill must meete a death,   30
Yea ev'n Princes (Gods) doe owe,
Heav'n at last a losse of breath.

Since then borne to die are Kings,
Mortalls hast your lives to mend,
For noe meaner mortall things   35
Are exempt, or free from end.

On Immortalitie.

Vp my soule, why slugg'st thou heere?
Why art thus press'd downe with feare?
Let noe earthly pleasure bend
Thee, from thy more noble end;
Divine thou wert made, and free,   5
And thy end Eternitie:
Spott not then thy selfe with drosse,
Nor thy rich creation crosse,
But arise, vp, and aspire
To the bright, celestiall quire,   10
There with pure devotion singe
Prayses, to th'Almighty Kinge;
There, all truth, all virtue growes,
There, are pleasures that would pose
Arithmeticke it selfe, there still   15
Perpetuall ioy the heart doth fill:
Sorrow is exil'd from thence,
There, inhabites innocence;
Then, if there be thine intent,
Strive for to be innocent.   20

On Christ's Passion.

What graceles wretch betray'd his gracious Lord?
Lord 'twas my sinnes, not Iudas soe abhorr'd.

Who scourg'd, who buffeted, and spitt vpon
The Lord of Life? Lord 'twas my sinnes alone.

What Devill thus bethorn'd the glorious face   5
Of heavens greate Kinge? only my selfe it was,

Each thorne that wounded his most lovely head,
Was by my crimes alone procured.

For me He sweate i'th'garden drops of bloud,
For me the Crosse was thought for him too good.   10

I was that Soldier that did pierce his side,
His precious side; and for my sinnes He di'd.

Another.

Whom seeke ye sinners, Iesus? know that I
Am he you seeke; behold me, I am nigh
To all that truely seeke me: But what rage
Hath forc'd you arm'd to seeke me? disingage
Your better iudgments, and you'l quickly find   5
I never was to Penitents vnkind.
Dar'st thou false Judas with a treacherous kisse
Betray thy lovinge Lord? have I for this
Not only made thee mine, but giv'n to thee
My purse in keepinge? hop'st thou to scape free   10
After such falshood? griefe, dispaire, and woe
For this will meete thee: Well, behold I goe
Whither you'l leade me, though I could have showne
My might, and Angells to my ayd call'd downe.
Whither you wicked rout, ô whither will   15
You dragge this innocent Lambe? for what greate ill
Doe you thus hale him? impious wretches speake,
Why smite you him that might you iustly beate?
What cruelty is this? can you doe this
To him that pardon begges for your amisse?   20
Canst thou ô Herod soe vniustly scorne
(Thee, and thy soldiers to) a man forlorne,
Forlorne for thee, and for them all oppress'd?
What madnes hath ye Scribes, ye Priests possess'd?
Art thou a Iudge ô Pilate, (set to kill   25
Such as transgresse by a notorious ill)
And is thy doome his death in whom erewhile
Thy selfe confess'd that thou didd'st find noe guile?
Must his life (offered) the attonement be,
And his bloud Herod reconcile, and thee?   30
O bloudie friendship, could your mortall strife
Be reconcil'd by nought but his deere life?

Fear'st thou not Pilate? think'st thou that the eye
Of heaven is blind on thy impiety?
Canst thou beleeve perverted iustice shall   35
Not be severely punish'd, meete a fall
For such an one as he? If any shall
Henceforth (authoriz'd) give wronge indgment, call
Him Pilate, and let his perverted will
For doinge wronge be punish'd with like ill.   40
Happie Cyrene, happier Simon, thou
Of all the rest (though forc'd) didd'st (faintinge) bowe
Vnder his Crosses weight, each humbled soule
Will envy thee thy load, and wish to houle
Vnder thy burthen; but content must be   45
Only to leave the happines to thee.
But hearke, me-thinkes a strange confused noise
I heare, all baulinge with a clamourous voice
Let him be crucifi'd, 'tis fit he die;
Dispatch ye Officers, him crucifie.   50
Se, se how busie his Tormentours be;
Some healpe to hale him vp, another, he
Is ready to stretch out and hold his armes,
Whil'st one (more cunninge then the rest in harmes)
Above doth naile his hands, the whil'st belowe   55
Another nayles his feete, (skilfull I trowe
In such like devill-practises) some 'bove his head
Doe fixe a scornefull writt, all wish him dead
And yet without a fault: The soldiers to
(Busie in castinge lotts) his garments doe   60
'Mongst them divide; whilst he requites all this
With *Father pardon them their greate amisse*
For they are ignorant, and little know
Their ill, then pardon them deare Father doe.
And least he might be by the wiser few   65
Thought (as indeed he was) to be most true,
Two condemn'd wights (guilty of all pollution)

Must be companions in his execution;
A happinesse too greate for mortall breath,
To be associates with him in his death,   70
And that thou truely foundst repentant thiefe
Receivinge pardon for soe little griefe.
O cruell hearts can you (for all this) se
Me thus tormented for your sinnes, and ye
And not afford me pittie? knowe that none   75
Ever such sorrow felt as I have knowne,
Yea even the fiercenes of my Fathers ire,
For nothinge lesse your scarlet crimes require.
And is all this for me,! and shall I dare
To se thee thus, and not let fall one teare   80
For thee, and for my sinnes? O graunt thy grace
That they may trickle from my heart apace,
And never stint, till by the bloud of thee
I am made Cleane from my impuritie.

On the strange apparitions at Christ's death.

What strange vnvsuall prodigie is heere,
The height of day and yet noe Sunne appeare,
Nothinge but darkenes to be seene? what fright
Hath caus'd the day thus to be turn'd to night?
Sure th'old Chaos, or the day of Doome   5
Heaven, and earth's fabricke to dissolve is come,
For se graves open, and in ev'ry streete
The dead are seene to stand vpon their feete,
Nor is the Temple safe, its Vale in sunder
Is rent, by a prodigious clappe of thunder,   10
And all disorder'd is: Gods Sonne is dead
Noe marvell then, the Sunne doth hide its head.
Blacke death hath ceiz'd vpon the God of light,
'Tis equall then day mourne in sable night.
Nor is it fitt the graves should peopled be   15
With dead, when earth receives eternitie.
The Temple's vale must rent in pieces be
Least there should want a winding-sheete for thee.
Nor is 't a wonder that all things doe lie
Disorder'd, and are sicke when God can die.   20

On his sweate on mount Olivet.

Marke how the dropps doe trickle downe his face,
Vnvsuall drops; behold with what a grace
A heavenly grace he prayes, but yet his heart
You may perceive is pain'd with extreame smart;
His sweate's meere bloud, and in such plenty flowes   5
In such greate tricklinge dropps as plainly showes
That nothinge but the whole worlds desp'rate sinne
Could have made God in such a case have beene.

On Christ crown'd with thornes.

Know you what he is you scorne,
Whom it is you crowne with thorne?
        In his eye
        You may 'spie
Perfection, and Eternitie: 5

Know each drop of bloud you shead
From his lovely face, his head
        And each thorne
        He hath borne
Will your condemnation be.   10

Marke but how in spight of paine,
He all mildnes doth retaine,
        What a grace
        Hath his face,
Farre-transcendinge humane beauty.   15

These pure droppes will purge away
All the drosse from breathinge Clay
        In each part
        If to th'heart
With fayth, they be appli'd, and duty.   20

Cease ye bloudie Iewes to rend
Any more his flesh, and mend,
        Quickly mend,
        Least your end
Doome you die perpetuallie   25

For 'tis Christ you thus doe scorne,
Iesus, whom you platt with thorne
        Then beware
        How you dare
Scorne, and bethorne Eternitie.   30

On the Spirit adulterated by the flesh.

My soule cleaveth to the dust, Quicken thou me—Psalm: 119:ve:25.

How doe I spinne my tyme away
   In caringe how to gett
   Vngodly wealth, and frett
     My selfe to sweate,
As if thou Lord had'st meant this Clay   5
Noe after life, noe reck'ninge day.

What graceles foole would love his earth
   Soe, as with all his might
   To pamper with delight
     The same 'gainst right,   10
Forgettinge his divine soules birth
Was nobler, and of greater worth?

Thou Lord did'st frame this soule of mine
   Only to honour thee,
   Not basely fond to be   15
     Of vanitie,
Vnflesh it then, and soe refine
It Lord it may be all divine.

Quicken my dull-droopinge-spiritt
   That it may praise thy name,   20
   Cleanse it from sinne and blame,
     Take from it shame.
Grante that by my Saviours meritt
Eternitie it may inherite.

Let it not grovelinge lie press'd downe   25
   With earth, but mount, and gaine
   An everlastinge raigne,
     Let it retaine
Noe drosse, and when it shall have throwne
Its cover off, graunt it a crowne.   30

The Summons.

O yes, sinfull flesh come heere,
'Fore the Iudgement seate appeare,
  The Court is set
  And will not let
Any scape vnfin'd that come   5
  Not soone away,
  Make noe delay
Least you hasten on your doome.

O yes, hearke y'are call'd agen,
To appeare delay not then   10
  For you cannot,
  Nor you sha'not
'Scape from this greate Session,
  The Iudge is kind,
  And you will find   15
Most favour by confession.

O yes, ô yes; this's the last
Summons, the third call make hast,
  It is in vaine
  To thinke t'refraine   20
From this greate appeale, this Call,
  Therefore beware,
  And you prepare
For this Session generall.

The Arraignment.

Sinfull soule come forth and stand
    To the Barre,
Thereon lay thy guilty hand;
    Never stare,
Nor thinke thou canst escape vntride from hence,   5
Guilt must be punish'd, pardon'd Innocence.

Stand to th'barre I say, your feare
    Doth betray
Your guilt, and th'accusers are
    Heere to say   10
And sweare their Accusation is most true;
But first th'indictment shall be read to you.

The Indictment.

You are indicted Sinner (by the name
Of desp'rate sinner) for your want of shame
     And first the ill
Of your first-parents disobedience,
      Their corrupt will   5
You have retayn'd, their losse of Innocence
    You stand indicted for,
     Beside, the score
Of your owne faults doth rise to such a height,
The Audit's greater then you can sett streight.   10

Can you deny how you have swollen with Pride?
And how notoriouslie, how oft y'ave Li'de?
     How your delight
Is in base envy?, and in swillinge drincke
     Both day and night?   15
Your bloudie hands crie guilt, nor must you thinke
    You can your Murder hide;
     Next these doe ride
Beastly Adultery, ill-manner'd Theft
Nor at these seaven scarlett crimes ha'y'left.   20

These, with a number numberlesse beside
Of lesser crimes that cannot be deni'd
     Are of that rout
Which we Commission call, and will appeare
     Without all doubt   25
Exceedinge heynous, next to these there are
    Sinnes of a lesser kind,
     Yet you will find
That when their weight, and number comes to viewe
Offended Iustice will not pardon you.   30

These briefely you shall heare, as first how oft

Have you the naked cloth'd? or with your soft
      And tender love
Reliev'd the sicke, and weake? how often fed
      Such as would move 35
With their leane cheeks the stones be turn'd to bread?
      Or have you ever lent
          The innocent
Your needfull healpe? or sheltred from distresse
The forlorne widdowes, and the fatherles? 40

These, and the like crimes are Omission nam'd:
For wilfull, and Presumptuous sinnes y'are blam'd
      Next, and accus'd
Of both which infinites y'ave committed
      And God abus'd; 45
Particulers of each I have omitted
      To treate of, 'cause the thronge
          Would be too longe.
And last, the crimes that your guilt more enhance,
Are of Infirmitie, and Ignorance. 50

All these forenam'd, with thousand thousands more
To Gods dishonour done are on your score,
      Against the peace,
The Crowne, and dignitie o'th'King of Kings.
      For your release 55
Can you say ought, or what for all these sinnes
      Can you expect but hell?
          Then quickly tell
By whom you will be tri'd,? Guilty, or noe?
Confesse, your guilt noe other Plea can showe. 60

The Regenerate sinners plea.

What though I guilty be of all these crimes
        And more
Then you accuse me of, a thousand times,?
        As I confesse
           My score   5
        Is nothinge lesse,
Yet let me not without my Tryall die,
But let my cause God, and my Country trie.

The Iury's mercifull, and they will find
        My soule   10
By th'precious bloud, and wounds o'th'Lambe refin'd,
        Nor will the Iudge
           The roule
        Of mercy grudge,
For Christ the Altar of the Crosse hath tri'd   15
For me, to wash away my guilt he di'd.

The vnregenerate Sinners plea.

I would have mercy to, but cannot aske,
    I know noe begginge way,
        I'l then assay
        Another taske,
     And cunningly abuse   5
The Court, and Iustice and my selfe excuse.

Pray heare me speake, I meane not to confesse
    The guilt I never knew,
        False, and vntrue
        Yea reasonlesse   10
    Is your accusation,
I'l prove my selfe one of another fashion.

The world it selfe with all its pompe, and state
    Shall testifie for me,
        The flesh shall be   15
        My test, I hate
    Such acts, nor did give way
Ever, to such enormous crimes as they;

And good (I hope) and credible's their proofe,
    Such as you'l not denie: 20
        I cannot lye
        For my behoofe
    I have reliev'd, and fed
The hungrie soule, the sicke have cherished,

The naked cloth'd, all this, and much beside   25
    For Christians I have done,
        And God-the-Sonne;
        Let me be tri'd
    And let my Country have,
And God, the hearinge of my cause I crave.   30

The veredict.

The Bill, and Proofes on eyther side
   W'ave heard at full,
And find we cannot disannull
   Th'offenders pride,
    Both have done ill,   5
    But not alike in will;
The first hath sinn'd, but hath confess'd
His guilt longe since, and thereby gotten rest.

The last hath trespass'd to, but in
   A higher kind,   10
And with a proud and stubborne mind
   Denyes his sinne,
    We find beside
    His witnesses have di'd
Their guilt, in as deepe graine as he,   15
And (though not yet) shall shortly punish'd be.

The good h'ath done for Christ, and his
   Is but pretence
Of good, and craftie impudence,
   Nor doth all this   20
    Excuse, but adde
   To what he hath done bad,
And 'twere a wronge to innocence
To creditt those guilty o'th'same offence.

We find the Bill, and Test to be   25
   In all most true
And th'last offenders life t'be due
   Eternallie
    To hells damn'd pitt,
    The other we acquitt,   30
Soe we say all, but doe referre
Vs, and the cause, to th'Bench, and Iusticer.

The Sentence.

Let all the pris'ners stand forth to the barre
    But let all the guilty stand
    By themselves on the Left-hand:
Set also those, that tri'd, and freed are
    On the dexter-hand and se   5
    Till sentence passe all silent be.

First then to you whose penitence hath sav'd
    You from an eternall end,
    I doe vnto you Commend
These glorious crownes, for that you have behav'd   10
    You well, come bless'd soules and se
    The Kingdomes are prepar'd for ye.

Next to the guilty (with vnwillinge heart
    And relentinge soule for you)
    Since you have beene soe vntrue,   15
Without delay you must from hence depart,
    And receive your wicked hire
    With Sathan in hells livinge fire

Nor can you thinke the Iudgment's too severe
    Since your triall equall was,   20
    And your crimes have to your face
Beene too truely proov'd, nor will sorrow e'r
    Availe now, too late you crie
    The doome is pass'd, and you must die.

Goe then you cursed and receive your hire   25
With Sathan in hells ever-burninge fire.

An Appendixe.

Offended Iustice in this Court's the Crier,
The Devill is the Clerke (not of the Peace)
To frame th'Indictment, and will never cease
To vrge th'extreamitie of Law, the Trier
       And Iudge of this Offence   5
       Is righteous Innocence;
       Conscience th'Accuser is
         Who in this Triall
       Will all excuses misse,
         Take noe denyall.   10
Bless'd Truth, and Peace, with Piëtie, and Mildnes
Mercy, and Pittie, virtue, and Humilitie,
Grace, and Love doinge good with all agilitie,
Firme-Hope, and savinge Faith-eschewinge vilenes,
       These are the Grand-Inquest.   15
       Accordinge to the Test,
The Foreman-Truth the Pris'ners guilt doth tender,
Soe they say All, the Sinfull soule's th'Offender
Th'Executioner Death waites but till
The Sentence passe to send the Soule to hell.   20

On Prayer.

How sweetly that harmonious musicke strikes mine eare,
  Me-thinks the chime of every stringe I heare
    Doth captivate my Hearings sence,
      By Concords influence,
        As if it meant   5
          To rent
    That sence from all the rest,
    And would, were I not press'd
  With such a heavy load of crimes,
  That groanes, and sighes my musicke chimes.   10

And though these grones, and sighes such heavy musicke are—
  Yet such the musicke is 'twill pierce the eare
    Of the Almighty, and will presse
      Into his sight, nor cease
        Vntill he graunt   15
          My plaint,
    Prayer hath such a force,
    'Twill breed in God remorse,
  Such silent hearty prayers will drawe
  Where noe force bends, nor feare can awe.   20

Shall then the sinfull soule for sighes, and grones receive
  Forgivenes of his sinnes? ô then bereave
    My stubborne heart of all that may
      Hinder it thus to pray;
        Purge from my will   25
          All ill,
    And let it not give o'r
    Groninge till it be sore,
  And the barren-stony-matter
  Dissolve to flesh in teary water.   30

Another.

Art thou sicke? the way to health
Is gotten by the precious wealth
Of pure prayer, that's the phisicke
Will cure thee of thy sinfull tisicke:
Art thou poore? the way to raise   5
Thy ruin'd state's by prayer, and praise;
Hath close bonds thy body pin'd?
Hunger grip'd thy very mind?
Hast thou plaid with God the Thiefe?
Is thy conscience pinch'd with griefe?   10
Do'st thou feare th'eternall fire
Of Hell, or would'st to heaven aspire?
All shall happie thee by prayer,
That bless'd Incense to the chayre
Of th'Almightie shall ascend,   15
And thy votes to him commend;
That will presse beyond the thronge
And drowne the musicke, and the songe
Of heaven it selfe, that alone
Shall bringe thee pardon from the throne.   20
Grante me grace then Lord that I
May with fervent prayer crie
To thy goodnes, and ne'r cease
Till from thee I've purchas'd peace.

On Death.

The more I thinke, the more I may,
How soone we passe from hence away
To people graves, how fraile's our clay.

A thousand wayes we have from hence,
Against the smallest worme noe fence   5
Can save vs from Deaths residence.

Only one common way doth bringe
Into light this wretched thinge
Call'd man, Affliction's offeringe.

His cradle is a bed of death,   10
Each swooninge fitt a losse of breath,
Each flie can send him vnto Leth'.

Each moment's time enough to send
Him vntimely to his end,
And deny him time to mend.   15

Let vs then prepared be
To meete death when'ever he
Shall call vs to eternitie.

Another. [I]

My bed's my grave, my grave's my bed,
My sleepe's like death, I sleepe but dead;
Stretch'd out at length I sleepinge lie,
And am but stretch'd out when I die;
My flesh is pallid made by feare,   5
And pale's the culler death doth weare;
My sleepe, or swoone resembles death,
And death it selfe's but losse of breath;
My sheets I sleepe in seeme to me
Nought but my windinge-sheet to be.   10
When I am layd downe in my bed,
Me-thinks I then seeme coffined.
The Clocke doth seeme my passinge-bell,
The Cocks-crowinge my funerall peale,
And each thinge in a severall fashion   15
Presents death to my meditation.

Another. [II]

Why to our clay was life allow'd, and breath?
                    For death.
And must both good, and bad and all sorts die?
                    Sure I.
Can we not then avoyd death's fatall blowe?   5
                    Noe, noe.
When we were borne what did we hither bringe?
                    No thinge.
And when we parte hence shall we nothinge have?
                    A grave.   10
Is then a grave the most we shall retaine?
                    Greate gaine.
What gaine's soe greate may meritt all be given?
                    Heaven.
Have we then after death a further blisse?   15
                    O yes.
And how to it will seeme our worldly losse?
                    Meere drosse.
And will that blisse for evermore endure?
                    Most sure.   20
Who is it that these blessings will afford?
                    The Lord.
What sort of mortalls tast these pleasures must?
                    The Iust;
Only the Iust, what must the rest then doe?   25
                    Die to.
And beinge dead in what place doe they dwell?
                    In Hell.
And have they there a ioyfull happie raigne?
                    All paine.   30
Those then live ever, but these truely die?
                    I, I.

He that will ever live, and never end
            Must mend.
Grante Lord once dead I rise to life agen,   35
            Amen.

On Drunckenesse.

How ill doth he deserve the name of man,
    Lesse Christian,
    Who doth abuse
Gods image by excesse in common vse,

For moderation is approv'd at least   5
    By every beast,
    Yet man alone
To whom reason given was admitts of none.

Men of that bruitish rancke I meane, who thinke
    Noe life to drincke,   10
    Whose tubbs ever
Are emptie, bottomles, and sated never,

Who rise to swill, and glutt with all delight
    Their appetite,
    At noone-of-night,   15
Retire, disgorge, and snore till morninge light.

These only weare mens outsides, but at touch
    Prove nothinge such,
    The least excesse
Is gods dishonour, sinne to Holinesse.   20

O who would then his vnderstandinge kill
    By base selfe will,?
    Or love t'exceed
In what in beasts doth detestation breed.

Another.

'Tis not the quaffinge off of healthes vntill
    Thou doe thine owne health kill,
Nor will thy druncken reelinge ever gett
    Thee an eternall seate,
For know the Kinge of heaven hates the stincke   5
    Of all exceedinge drincke,
All the whole druncken spewinge swinish rout
    Shall be from heaven shutt out.
Yea God shall spew them from his sacred mouth,
    And an eternall drouth   10
Shall gnawe, and gripe their very soules who dare
    Slight the Almighties feare.
And iust it is the drunckard still should thirst,
    Who while he lived durst
Exceed in drincke, and water be deni'd,   15
    Whom tunnes ne'r satisfi'd.
But if thou needs wilt drincke, seeke to obtaine
    The drincke that n'er againe
Thou may'st be thirstie, pray, and Christ shall give
    Drincke shall make thee ever live.   20

On Marriage.

Marriage is that sacred tie
That ioynes two lovinge hearts in one,
Nor can love be parted ever,
Though bodies farre asunder lie,
Firme affections strength alone   5
Is such as death could conquer never,
For death can only part the clay,
Soe takes but the worst halfe away.

But divine Loves mansion, is
Seated in the starry heaven,   10
And admits of noe mutation,
Its pure ayerie soares to blisse,
And by God alone was given
To inhabite that bless'd station:
Who sayth he loves, and changes seate,   15
His flame's but an adulterate heate.

Such hearts then as are ioyn'd by love
Are first in heaven married;
In vayne doe mortalls then deny
To such the marriage bed to prove,   20
Or hope they can be varyed
From th'old, and new affection trie;
For whom God once hath ioyn'd in heart
Let sinfull mortalls feare to part.

Marriage hath ever beene esteem'd   25
An honour'd tie, and cheifely such
Whose chaster-virgin-beds ne'r knew
But one live love, and dead him deem'd
Worthy alone t'be lov'd soe much
That they would ne'r admit a new,   30
And happie is that marriage bed,
Where both are truely married.

Happie indeed, but farre more bless'd
Is that rich soule whose love is plac'd
Vpon the God of love, and he   35
Is pleas'd to marry to his rest,
Where in heaven it shall be grac'd
With honour to eternitie;
This indeed's the happiest bride
That ever sate her Spowse beside.   40

And thus th'Almightie's pleas'd to wed,
When as the soule vnto him sues
With fervent love, he ne'r denies
But straight she shall be marryed,
God will not coy it, nor refuse   45
The lovinge soule that to him flies;
O sacred rite, ô honour'd life,
Since God is pleas'd to take a wife.

And art thou pleas'd to fall in love
With that sicke soule that seekes to thee   50
In fervent love, and earnestnes?
Grante then mine may truely move,
And to th'Lambe may marri'd be
In perpetuall happinesse:
He who's thus sped, and wed shall ne'r   55
Need a separation feare.

On Beautie.

When I behold one faire
Me-thinks I spie
Somwhat soe like the maiestie
Of heaven, I admire
The brightnes of the fire,   5
And thinke that rare
Should not containe ought ill, but be
Noe lesse then what it seemes to me.

Who would expect to find
In such a face   10
Soe Angel-like, soe full of grace
Ought but a mind as free,
And pure, as pure may be
With virtue lin'd!
Darke deeds i'th'darke are chiefely done,   15
And bad ones only feare the Sunne.

The face was only made
Such, that the heart
Might truely be in every part
With grace, and goodnes dress'd,   20
This will be surely bless'd
Though beautie fade;
A virtuous inside God best loves,
This is the beauty he approves.

The outward beauty then   25
I'l love, but soe
As while within doth virtue growe,
And but admire the face,
As a peculiar grace
Bestow'd on men.   30
Lord let my heart be faire to thee
Noe matter what my outside be.

On Anger.

Why should I frett me, or be crosse
　　At any mortall losse,
　　Or rage my reason blind?
　　　　Since nought belowe
Is worth the anger of a virtuous mind,　　　　　　　5
　　　　Passion doth showe
Too much of youthfull heate, but small
Discretion, and true iudgement none at all.

Suppose my ioy's by death exil'd
　　In a friend, wife, or child　　　　　　　　　10
　　Such as could be never
　　　　Their equall found,
Shall I be strucke into a sullen fever?
　　　　Or is the ground
Become my bed, who but now had　　　　　　　15
More wealth, then might have made an hundred mad?

Am I with sicknes grip'd within,
　　With sores pain'd beyond the skin,
　　Are all pleasant houres lost,
　　　　And I alone　　　　　　　　　　　20
Seeme only borne to be in all things cross'd
　　　　And live to mone,
Yet the best comfort I could gaine
By rage, were but addition to my paine.

Let me not then with Ionah be　　　　　　　25
　　Displeas'd thou hast from me
　　The shadow t'a'n away,
　　　　But let my zeale
Storme, and be grieved at my sinfull clay
　　　　When it shall steale　　　　　　　30
　　Thy glory, and dishonour thee
By sinne; then raginge let my passion be.

On the names Iesus, Christ, Emanuell.

I n vayne we strive to cure our griefe by art,
E ase, and redresse come only from above,
S alvation's sent even by the Fathers love
V nto the sinsicke world, its fester'd heart
S hall find most ease in balme of Gilead. 5

C hrist is that sacred oyle from whom alone
H ealth may be purchas'd, and Salvation,
R ich in his mercy, what in vs is bad
I s by his passion purg'd, and purifi'd.
S uch sufferings, such love as he hath showne 10
T he world, except in him was never knowne.

E ach soule repentant he hath Deifi'd;
M an wholly lost in wickednes, and sinne
A lone by him, and by his death is freed,
N one ever could have wrought this wondrous deed, 15
V nlesse this Saviour God himselfe had beene,
E ven the Sonne-of-God this Saviour is,
L ord, and th'anoynted oyntment of our blisse.

On Lazarus rais'd from death.

Where am I, or how came I heere, hath death
       Bereav'd me of my breath,
         Or doe I dreame?
     Nor can that be, for sure I am
These are noe ensignes of a livinge man,   5
       Beside, the streame
        Of life did flie
From hence, and my bless'd soule did soare on high;
       And well remember I,
       My friends on eyther hand   10
        Did weepinge stand
        To see me die;
Most certaine then it is my soule was fled
Forth of my Clay, and I am buried.

These linnens playnly shew this cave did keepe   15
       My flesh in its dead sleepe,
        And yet a noise
     Me-thought I heard, of such strange force
As would have rais'd to life the dullest coarse,
        Soe sweete a voice   20
        As spight of death
Distill'd through every veyne a livinge breath,
       And sure I heard it charge
       Me by my name, ev'n thus
         O Lazarus   25
        Come forth at large,
And se nought hinders, I will straightway then
Appeare, (though thus dress'd) ere it call agen.

Was't my Redeemer call'd, noe marvell then
       Though dead, I live agen,   30
        His word alone

Can rayse a soule, though dead in sinne,
Ready the grave of hell to tumble in
   High as the Throne;
    In all things he   35
Is the true powerfull Eternitie:
   Since thou hast pleas'd to raise
   My body then, let my spirit
    Heav'n inherite
    And thee praise.   40
And let thy miracle vpon my clay
Prepare, and fitt me 'gainst the reck'ninge day.

My last will, and Testament.

Not sicke in body but in mind most free,
        Of perfect sence,
    Choice health, and apt capacitie,
        Willinge from hence
    To parte, though not prepared soe   5
        As fitt to goe
Without due preparation hence to death,
I'th'name of God I thus my all bequeath,

And first my earth vnto its proper place
        Earth I allott   10
    Wishinge a grave, and yet such grace
        Regardinge not,
    My vaine delights the world me gave
        The world shall have,
All carnall lust, and sensuall desire   15
The sinfull flesh (as its iust due) shall heire.

All heynous crimes, my impious blasphemy,
        My cursinge to,
    My lyinge, and hypocrisie,
        With all I doe   20
    Or ever have done, wondrous ill,
        It is my will
The Devill take, as only due to him,
For by his craft I have thus wicked beene.

My guilty conscience I bequeath in fee   25
        To wicked men,
    Yet wish to shunne they carefull be
        The Devills den,
    For though he promise faire, the gaine
        Will be but paine,   30
Strange is that griefe for which was ne'r found cure

More strange hells torments that for ever 'dure.

The flesh, with what belongs to sinfull earth
          Thus giv'n away,
    My soule that from above tooke birth   35
          I give for aye
    To heaven, and God who gave it me,
          Dispos'd to be
Accordinge to his blessed will, in hope
He will invest it with a glorious cope.   40

To God-the-Sonne (who with his precious bloud
          Hath me redeem'd)
    My true repentance, and what good
          May be esteem'd
    Mine by his merits, I bequeath   45
          Him; for his death
I never can with penitence requite
Enough, his bloud alone hath made me white.

My will is likewise, that the Holy-Spirit
          Please to receive   50
    All thoughts, words, works I doe inherite
          And holy leave,
    To th'rich relligious leave will I
          My Charitie,
To th'honest poore (who are by griefe press'd downe)   55
My hope, the riches of a glorious Crowne.

Fayth I bequeath to the weake Christian,
          To the Saints blisse,
    To th'meeke humility, who never can
          Bless'd Kingdomes misse,   60
    To all the good, all goodnes still
          I leave and will,
And last to order all, th'Almighty power
(Of this my will) I make Executour.

On Time.

Most fitly Poets vnto Time applie
  The vse of Sithe and wings,
To shew how suddenly he hence doth flie,
  And yet all mortall things
He in this swiftnes doth inforce to die,   5
  And to confusion brings,
And what this day, this houre, growes, and lives,
Next minutes moment vnto death he gives.

Each yeare, moneth, weeke, day, houre, make little stay
  But still give place to new,   10
And every minute flies, and posts away
  And others doe pursue.
Trees, hearbs, birds, beasts, have a determin'd day
  Which they cannot eschew,
And all things mortall die, and are renew'd   15
By tyme, and subiect to vicissitude.

Yea man himselfe the whole worlds Emperour
  Is subiect vnto fate,
Nor can avoyd swift tymes devouringe power
  With all his pompe, and state,   20
And time itselfe shall in the end devoure
  Itselfe, and meete a date.
The longest day's at last o'rspread with night,
And darkenes banish'd is by th'Sunnes cleare light.

Since every houre then, and moment may   25
  Be every mortalls last,
Greate care we ought to have least we betray
  Th'immortall part by wast,
For though the body die, and passe away
  The soule can never tast   30
Death like the flesh, but eyther lives in paine

Perpetuall, or in endles ioy doth raigne.

I'l ever pray then that I soe may be
      Prepared, that when'e'r
Death takes my clay hence to eternitie,   35
      I may without all feare
Welcome that happie houre that makes me free
      Of all my worldly care;
For who the death o'th'righteous would die
On earth must labour to live righteouslie.   40

On Deformitie.

Dull mortalls measure by th'externall hue
      The beauty hid within,
          And groslie deeme
That an apparent truth which outward shew
          Doth seeme t'assure,   5
But God the searcher of all hearts with sight
          Most wise, and pure
Is not deceiv'd with beauties glim'ringe light,
      And though the hypocrite
          Be seeminge right,   10
And with a shew of holines beguile
The world, yet Ioue doth know him false, and vile.

The fairest face oft owes the foulest heart,
      And doth (though goodnes showe)
          Noe virtue owe,   15
And often though deform'd i'th'outward parte
          A heart we find
Season'd with grace, and heavenly goodnes soe
          As showes a mind
Where noe deformitie, or vice doth growe,   20
      Poore is that beauties grace
          Then, that's all face,
The virtuous inside's beautyes puritie,
Although deform'd, and foule the outside be.

All outsides then or faire, or foule shall be   25
      (While I none other knowe
          But what they showe)
Alike esteem'd, and valued by me
          Vntill I find
In foulenes virtue, or in beauty vice,   30
          For 'tis the mind

Alone, is beautious, or deform'd to th'wise;
    If then my outward part
       Be foule, my heart
I'l strive to beautifie with grace, if white,   35
Outside, and inside strive to make alike.

On Pride.

Pride still presumes how foule soe'r it be,
Itselfe the comli'st in the companie
      And thinks whatsoe'r it doe
      Cannot but merit praise
      And be rewarded to   5
      And will its owne worth raise
      Though by anothers losse,
      It basely still detracts,
      And earnestly doth crosse
      Anothers honest acts,   10
      Esteeminge nought well done
      But what's its worke alone.
It loves noe neighbour but the flatteringe beast
Or such as will be vnderlings at least.

Th'ambitious Lady who is never fine   15
Vnlesse i'th'wealth of Kingdomes she doe shine
      Would hate that costly dresse
      And thinke it poore, and base,
      Should any seeme noe lesse
      Costly then shee i'th'place,   20
      Soe strange a nature pride
      Hath, that it would have all
      Like it, yet will abide
      None as a Corrivall;
      It best affects command,   25
      And rule, at any hand.
Nor is 't a wonder, for in heaven it first
Tooke birth, and vie with God himselfe it durst.

This was that fatall sinne that caus'd divorce
'Twixt God, and Angells whose rebellious course   30
      God iustly doom'd to be

Bereav'd, and dispossess'd
Of heav'n, and eternitie
And everlastinge rest.
Had haughty Lucifer   35
Not sought t'aspire above
His maker, he had there
Beene happie in his love,
But when he needs would be
Above his God, then he   40
Was iustly throwne from happines to hell,
Since he soe proudly durst 'gainst God rebell.

And is this pride then such an iniurious evill,
To cause an Angell to become a Devill?
If Angells thus may fall,   45
The priviledge of men
Is lesse, more apt to thrall,
How carefull ought we then
Be to avoyd this sinne,
God will the meeke exalt,   50
And such as humble beene,
But this aspiringe fault
Shall ne'r meete other gaine
Then everlastinge paine:
O then let mortalls shunne this fearefull evill, 55
Least they hells torments suffer with the devill.

But if we must be proud of ought, graunt Lord
We may reioyce in thy most holy word.
Let our pride, and glory be
Of noe vaine, noe worldly thinge,   60
But let vs exult in thee
And thy crosse eternall Kinge,
Let vs suffer all disgrace
Proudly, that the world can lay,
And all sufferings imbrace   65

For thy sake, we humbly pray,
Let our pride, and glory be
In thy crosse alone, and thee.
Thus to be proud is glory, not a fault,
This pride shall God himselfe to heaven exalt.   70

On Humilitie.

Humility's a Vine, whose roote though earth
Seeme to lay clayme to, yet its branch aspires
High as the greate Iehovah's sacred quires,
And thither tends from whence it first tooke birth.
Faine it would be receiv'd by mortall clay   5
But cannot get admittance 'cause 'tis poore,
(Especially if pride be at the dore)
But is disgracefully driven thence away;
All sorts, all sexes shunne its conversacon,
Only the righteous love its cleanly fashion.   10

If to the Pallace it doth come for ayd,
It may be promis'd faire, but not let in,
Vnlesse it angells have good will to winne,
It shall be sure by all to be denai'd,
If 'monge the greate ones, greatnesse doth seldome take   15
Notice of humble things, the rich disdaine
Lowly acquaintance, 'lesse they bringe them gaine,
Cittizens hate it but for profit-sake,
If to the poore it come, 'tis like to find
Cold harbour there, yet they are lightly kind.   20

Thus every sorte doe thinke themselves disgrac'd
Let but Humility acquaintance claime
Of them, they tell her she is much to blame,
Yet by the virtuous shee's esteem'd, and plac'd
I'th'highest rancke, wisedome will still preferre   25
The humble soule above the common rout,
The sincere Christian's easili'st found out
By true humilitie, that badge will ne'r
Faile, nor be out of date, let me be knowne
Lord, by this badge of thine to be thine owne.   30

Profitt, and pleasure both this Angell brings,

Better then can the purest angell-gold
This, (more then all his miracles) hath told
The world, our Saviour Christ's the King of Kings.
'Tis this that makes men Angells, more then soe   35
Like God, yea gods themselves, by this alone
Th'are made Christ's partners i'th'eternall throne,
Plant then this herbe-of-grace, and make it growe
In my poore, barren heart ô Lord, that I
Only to heaven, and thee may fructifie.   40

On the life of Christ.

Ἀλλὲγορίκὴ

Who sayth, or thinks noe age did showe
     A blacke swan, let such knowe
      Poore Beth'lem did produce
       A bird more faire
Then any water, Rivulet, or sluce   5
       E'r knew, the ayre
Never was beate by any winge could showe
Such heavenly beauty as this bird did owe.

    This faire one from above tooke flight,
      And is i'th' breast more white   10
       Then e'r was any Swan.
        That part nor wind,
Nor sunne, nor any foule infection can
       Make t'alter kind:
His notes, and tunes were like his breasts pure shine,   15
Soe soft, and sweete the harmony's divine.

    Bless'd was the day that first did see,
      This bird of eternitie,
      The silver water Poe
       Or any River,   20
Such tunes, such harmony as this to showe
       In vaine endeavour
Of him the sweetest swannes that e'r did singe,
May heare, and learne when'er his voice doth ringe.

    Never before, nor since was found   25
      Any that could his sound
      Equall, much lesse outvie
       And yet to please
Only, he sunge not, but did willinge die
       For the disease   30
Of lesser birds vnworthy, he alone

For love, and note doth best deserve renowne.

    A sacred dirge before his death
        He tun'd, with such a breath
        Soe sweete, the like was ne'r   35
           Or heard, or sunge;
Whose sweetnes when they could not peere,
        The wicked thronge
In envy stopp'd his breath, in hope that then
They never more should be outsunge agen.   40

    They pack'd him from the earth indeed
        But could noe more, with speed
        To heaven he flew, since when
           Th'ave mourn'd his want,
But could they mourne till they were earth agen   45
        'Twere all too scant,
For earth hath lost him, but in heaven he sings
Crown'd, and copartner with the King of Kings.

    Yet soe, as hee's propitious still
        To such as labour will   50
        To learne his notes, it is
           His choyce delight
To meete with lesser birds, and swans that his
        Love would requite,
And willingly receive his heavenly fire,   55
And labour to make one in his choyce quire.

    Henceforth then let all the frie
        Of swans, and birds lay by
        All other tunes, and be
           By him alone   60
Taught, and instructed in his harmony,
        And every one
With his best skill, and musicke strive to raise,
And magnifie this swans immortall praise.

On his Birth.
A Pastorall.

Sophos.   Pastor.

Soph: Shepheards whither are you bound?
        What strange passetime have you found,
        That you make such hast away?
        With vs make a little stay,
        And declare the cause, and whither   5
        You flocke thus hastily together.

Past: Knowe then, wee this night have seene
        A strange vision on yond greene,
        As we there our flockes did watch,
        Least some wolfe a lambe should catch.   10
        A heavenly thinge with glory clad
        To vs all appear'd, and bad
        That we should to Beth'lem hie,
        Where a Babe we should espie
        In a manger layd, from whom   15
        Our redemption needs must come,
        And we thither goe, with ioy
        To behold this heavenly boy.
        And loe while I linger here
        My company are almost there,   20
        Wherefore I must hence away
        Soe farewell;

                    Soph: I preethee stay,
        We also have beheld from farre
        (In the East) a glisteringe starre,
        Which hath brought vs to adore   25
        This Child, and offer choycest ore,
        Spices, myrrhe, and franckincense,

Nor intend we to parte hence
Till our tribute we have payd,
Therefore Shepheard lend thine ayd   30
To direct vs soonest thither
And wee'l company together.

Past: Then come on apace, for I
Am loth to loose my Company,
Se the starre you spake now on   35
Appeares in this Horizon,
That will guide you, and I faine
Would o'rtake my friends againe,
Beside, the way you need not feare
To loose, for you are almost there;   40
I must hie me:

                    Soph: Doe not though
Gentle Shepheard from vs goe,
For behold thy mates attend
And are at their iourneyes end,
Se with what devotion they   45
Honour to this infant pay,
Hearke with what loud shoutes they raise
Heavens, and this Babies praise,
Se the starre hath left its pace
And is fix'd iust o'r the place,   50
Which confirmes vs this is he,
We have come soe farre to se,
And we thanke thee for thy paine;

Past: Mickle thanks to you againe.

Soph: Come let's then together bringe   55
Submissively, our offeringe,
That done, let the swaines, and we
With devout, and merry glee,
Helpe th'angelicall quire to raise
This holy Babe, this Saviours praise.   60

On his Birth-day.

Eternall ioy will best befit
    This sacred day,
Henceforth the yeare from it
    Shall be for aye
Begun, and ended; let none dare   5
    To worke hereon,
But with all reverence and feare
    Let this, or none
Knowe nought but hymnes, and sacred fire,
Since Angells deigne to fill the quire.   10

This first by them observed was
    A holy-day,
For that the Sonne was pleas'd to grace
    Our sinfull clay,
Sent hither by his Fathers love   15
    That soe he might,
Cloth'd with our flesh, our sins remove
    And make vs white,
Let this day then honour'd be
For him that liv'd, and di'de for thee.   20

On ioy.

Can ioy be where there doth dwell
Torment little lesse then hell?
    Or can this world afford
    More ioy then the poore word?
        Since all belowe   5
        'S but meerely showe
If one minutes ioy vs blesse
The next 'tis eyther none, or lesse
    How falsely then we call
    That ioy, is none at all,   10
        A light reliefe,
        From the worlds griefe.

False, and adulterate it is,
That is not a lastinge blisse,
    Heavens ioy hath true weight   15
    Earthly's but counterfeite,
        Let vs be wise
        Then, and despise
The worlds ioy, and fixe our hearts
On that blisse that never parts,   20
    And labour to obtaine
    A celestiall raigne,
        Free from annoy
        Where's all true ioy.

On Mourninge.

How little cause we have for mirth,
How comfortles our lives are heere,
The very moment of our birth
By shrieks, and cries doth make appeare,
Borne are we to a world of sorrow   5
Which is made greater every morrow.

Sorrow, and sinne doe vs conceive,
Once borne, in sinne-Originall
We are bewrapp'd, sinne doth bereave
Our lives, our happines, and all,   10
How longe soe'r we drawe our breath,
Our Cradle's sorrow to our death.

Comfort, and ioy we never see,
But as if in a glasse belowe,
Hope only of eternitie   15
Is all the blisse this life doth knowe,
And best men are of ioy debarr'd,
But what they looke for afterward.

How foolish then are they who spend,
Their lives in wanton vaine delights   20
And only pleasures doe attend,
Thereon consuminge dayes and nights,
For sorrow (wisest tongues have told)
Exceeds earths laughter manifold.

Delights like flatteringe friends doe lead   25
Vs through our lives to ruine, and
At deaths-dore leave vs, soe once dead
We fall into the Devills hand:
It adulates vs to annoy,
And robs vs of our after-ioy.   30

But mourninge (bless'd companion) still
Like deaths-head, or our passinge-bell,
Puts vs in mind to grieve our ill,
And by repentance keepe's from hell;
This sorrow makes the mourners bless'd,   35
And brings them to perpetuall rest.

This needs noe sackcloth, or clothes rent,
Noe fellow-mourners companie,
Nor any outward complement
To force salt water from the eye;   40
This mourning's ever best alone,
And would but of itselfe be knowne.

As borne in sorrow, let me still
Rather the mourninge life preferre,
Lord, that instructs me grieve my ill,   45
And rectifies me when I erre;
Clad my earth's life with sorrow round,
Soe that my after may be crown'd.

The Invitation.

Ho, behold each sinfull wight
The Lambe doth to his feast invite,
And he hath carefully prepar'd
Noe penitents shall be debarr'd,
But come with freedome to this feast,   5
Each one, a happie, welcome guest:
Rich, and poore, diseas'd, and sound,
Such as are in sorrow drown'd,
Miser, beggar, noble, Kinge,
If they but contrition bringe   10
Shall be welcome hither, and
Receive forgivenes at his hand.
This is such a pow'rfull meale
That (if eaten with true zeale
And resolv'd repentance, soe   15
To live as ne'r againe to knowe
The like transgressions) it will cleanse
The sin-sicke soule from all offence,
Then come hither, yet beware
That you soe prepared are   20
Before you come, and truely dress'd
With zeale, and sinne be soe repress'd
That Love, Humility, and grace
May in your hearts hold chiefest place.
To these ioyne holy abstinence,   25
True teares, pure pray'r for innocence.
Examine, purge, condemne, and trie
Your selves, soe as none aske you why,
Or how, you chanced hither come
Without the weddinge-garment on,   30
When guilty and convicted found,
Y'are ta'n and darknesse pris'ner bound.
Come, and welcome then together,
If preparation you bringe hither.

On the Lords Supper.

Foule I am and cannot tell
    How to purge me,
Sad I am yet dare not showe
    What doth vrge me,
Sicke I am, and would be well   5
    But doe not knowe
What member is most payned,
    Distress'd I am
    'Bove any man
Yet cannot tell where comfort might be gayned.   10

Christ's bloud is the sacred oyle
    To make thee white,
By his bloud (though ne'r soe sad)
    Thou may'st be light,
        And glad;   15
Hee's a salve can make thee smile
    Though ne'r soe bad,
And will soone thy sicknes cure,
    He thy distresse
    Will sure make lesse,   20
And he alone can comfort best assure.

He ordain'd the Sacrament
    Of his bodie,
And his blessed bloud did shead,
    And daign'd to die   25
For vs poore mortalls, innocent;
    (O blessed deed)
That we might be freed thereby
    (If obedient)
    From punishment,   30
Such goodnes show'd he that for vs did die.

Did then our Saviour seale
 A Covenant
With his life, and bloud for vs
  And shall he want   35
   From vs
Then, true, thankful hearts to deale
 Like righteous
Measure, ô let's leave off sinne,
  And once made white   40
  Ne'r act the like,
But still contenue stedfastly therein,
Least by his bloud in vayne w'ave purged beene.

To the Church.

Hayle, holy Mother of the Christian-band,
Thou sacred structure of th'Almightie's hand,
Still may thy honour live, thy beauty be
Fayre as the best of ages e'r did see;
May bless'd Peace keepe thee, and thy counsell bringe   5
Peace to thy lovers, victory to th'Kinge,
Let pow'rfull prayer be thy daylie guest,
And may thy sword destroy that Babel-beast
Sainted-ambition, may the feare of thee,
And love of virtue strangle Treachery: 10
If any devill seeminge-Christian dare
Wound thy soft bosome with a traytrous speare,
Or with pretended zeale defiance bringe
And prove a schismaticke against the Kinge,
Or sleight thy reverend Fathers, may they feele   15
Thornes in their hearts, or may the iuster steele
Of faithfull subiects cut them out a lawe,
Eyther by love, or feare to live in awe,
Safe be thy sacred treasures, may thy Friend
Iehovah-Elohim ever defend   20
Thy reverend Miters, and their Minor-band,
And may he please even with his owne right hand
To blesse with happines, and shield the King
And his race-royall; may thousand Angells bringe
Ayd 'gainst his foes; then shall thy honour live   25
In spight of all the blowes your foes can give.

A vowe.

With what rich offeringe shall I requite
      Thy goodnes Lord,
    Who hast beene pleas'd to call
      Me to thy board
Where I have freely fed, and beene from all   5
      My sinnes made white?
Thou in thy love hast fed me soe that I
Have eate th'eternall to eternitie.

All my pollution's purg'd, my wounds are whole
      By thee alone,   10
    Yet I have nought to pay
      But what's thine owne.
Instruct me then, and strengthen me I pray
      That from my soule
I may firme penitence, and thanks bestowe   15
Largely on thee to whom my all I owe.

Then will I pay thee with relligious feare
      Morninge, and night,
    The sacrifice of prayse,
      And pray'r, as right   20
And equall 'tis I should, and ever raise
      (That all may heare)
My voice, and ioy that to the world is come
Free pardon for all sinne by God-the-Sonne.

Thy wounds I'l mourne for that from me they came,   25
      Lament thy death,
    Pitty thy torments to
      That 'reav'd thy breath,
As oft as thinke on thee I will thus doe,
      Or see the same   30
Presented to me in the Sacrament,

Yet still reioyce that thou wert hither sent.

I'l blesse thy mercy that was pleas'd to bowe
      To flesh for me,
   And still thy love admire   35
      And humilitie,
Last I will ever love, and thee desire,
     All this I vowe
(Lend me but grace) most faythfullie to hold
To my lives end, as every Christian should.   40

A Dreame.

Sicke to the death, diseas'd past humane art,
I sought for ease to cure my wounded heart
But sought in vayne me-thought, for phisicks skill
Could minister small comfort to my ill,
And I grew worse; at last with some small hope   5
Of helpe, or ease at least, vnto the Pope
I made addresse, he tooke me into hand
And thrice with holy water bath'd me, and
Lav'd my pollution off, then he appli'd
Beads, crosses, crucifixes, and much more beside   10
Of the like kind, some Pater noster's to
And Ave Mari's, plaisters all that doe
Serve to drawe out the humours, then the oyle
Of extreame vnction is appli'd a while,
All pow'rfull med'cines, and in every part   15
Wrought their effects vnlesse 'twere in my heart.
Then was I dress'd into a shirt of haire,
Barefoote, and barelegg'd, and all else as bare
Only a coate, and coule: this purge thus dress'd,
And ta'n did serve to vsher in the rest,   20
And was administred to adapt me beare
The rest, with the more reverence, and feare:
Last, a stronge cordiall was administred
By th'Doctours selfe, Blessinge thrice doubled;
Thus plaster'd, phisick'd, and well purg'd i'th'purse 25
He left me, but of my disease much worse,
Not eas'd, but more tormented, more vnsound,
At last, not hopinge that there could be found
A med'cine could allay my desp'rate fever,
And therefore ready to dispaire for ever,   30
(For soe the wicked doctour wrought) at last
Me-thought when all my hope of helpe was pass'd

I was invited by a holy man
To a spirituall banquett, who soe wan
On my credulitie, that I resolv'd   35
Once more to trie conclusion, he dissolv'd
By pow'rfull charmes, and precious balsomes soe
The stone that 'bout my heart congeal'd did growe,
That I began to weepe, then he appli'd
My sinnes deserts, Gods anger, and he tri'd   40
Many corrodinge plaisters, after these
He gave me phisicke that soone gave me ease,
Gods bounteous mercy, his Sonnes passion to,
The Holy-Spiritt ready to vndoe
The subtle webs of sinne, he told me then   45
I must repentance vse, the how, and when;
Fayth, hope, and love he sayd I must imbrace
To helpe my better part to savinge grace,
This, and much more he taught, and then me-thought,
There was a righteous breastplate forthwith brought,   50
And put vpon me, and my right hand held
A flaminge sword, my left advanc'd a shield,
(The sword was that o'th'spirit, the shield of Faith)
Thus arm'd you must resistance make, he saith
'Gainst your stronge foes, the world, the flesh, and devill,   55
From whom (beinge arm'd thus) you need feare noe evill.
Salvations helmet likewise he put on
Vpon my head, and when he had soe done
I found my selfe me-thought more sound then e'r
Freed from my sicknes, and as free from feare,   60
Only the feare of beinge ill agen,
And then I 'wak'd, and did I say and then
O that this sleepe, and dreame had beene for ever,
Or had it pleas'd th'Almighty that it never
Had beene a dreame but earnest, ô how bless'd,   65
And happie had I beene thus arm'd, thus dress'd.

On Christ's wounded side, and the soldier.

What bloudie hand, what barbarous tygers heart
    Acted this part?
Was not his torment greate enough before
    But they must needs add more,
      And breathles his side gore? 5
O horrid cruelty! could any see
Death acted soe to th'life in his erection,
Sorrow to th'full, torments in dire perfection
    And not astonish'd be,
      Pitty at least 10
The dyinge grones of one soe sore oppress'd?

Did nature marke him out a man that did it,
    Now heaven forbid it,
But if of humane race, sure from the breast
    Of some infernall beast 15
    He drew it, and increas'd.
The noble soldier (though incens'd) will ne'r
Murder a yieldinge foe, and voyd of armes
Will strive to shield him from all fresh allarmes,
    And was there then noe feare 20
    Nor love of worth
In this, that soe ignoblie durst shew forth

His slender valour on one breathles, who
    Never deserv'd a foe,
Soldier enough th'ast done to cause thy name 25
    Be registred, thy fame
    Shall be eternall shame.
O see the chance, thy fatall hand hath lent
His side a wound, from which pure fountaine flowes
Two sorts of pow'rfull drincke to heale his foes 30
    Water, and bloud both meant

       Though not by thee
As sacred cordialls for integritie.

This water will (well-wash'd into thy heart)
      Purge every part,   35
Then take a plaister of this crimson gore
    To heale thy fester'd sore,
    And strive to sinne noe more.
Happie then hand, and heart that by one wound
Didd'st point thy selfe, and others out a way   40
To purge the sinne from their polluted clay,
    O how did love abound
      In him, that then
Suffer'd such things for vs base, sinfull men.

Graunt vs thy grace ô holy Christ, that we   45
May for thy sorrow mourne, be heal'd by thee.

On Povertie.

How'ever former ages, this we knowe
Ever most reverence, and respect doth showe
To those of greatest wealth, the better halfe
Of our respect we pay the golden calfe,
When as (perhaps) farre more perfection dwells   5
In one of lower rancke, and all things else
May there be more praiseworthy; yet vnlesse
God in his providence be pleas'd to blesse
(Though ne'r soe worthy otherwise) with store
Of Mannours, Lordships, Castles, and much ore,   10
He is nought sett by, but if rich he be
Though vitious, foole, deform'd, yet this is he,
This is that gaudy thinge whose every nod
Must be observ'd, and honour'd as a god,
Strange power of gold, when worth, and virtue be   15
Scorn'd, and contemn'd because in povertie.
Poore men may now a dayes a begginge goe
And get the whip for almes, or if not soe
Nought but a churlish answeare at the best,
Or else be scorn'd off with some bitter ieast.   20
O times, ô manners; hath th'Almighty pleas'd
To spare me wealth, and shall I see th'diseas'd,
Poore, naked, hungry, and such like distress'd
And not afford them helpe? these are the best,
And choicest of Gods care, himselfe will still   25
Se these provided for, and take it ill
Even to the height, if any one shall dare
Deny some portion of his guifts to share
To the poore needie, and did therefore give
Blessings to some, that such as these should live.   30
Shall I then covet wealth, mainteyne a whore
That will consume me more then twenty pore,

Ruine my better part, and therefore grind
The poore, cozen the widdowes, and ne'r mind
The needy orphants clamours, shall I reape   35
The corne another sow'd, labour to heape
Vp thousands by some indirect, vngodly course
And soe by beinge rich make my soule worse,
Defend me heaven, and though I inherit
Noe more, yet let me Lord be poore in spirit;   40
Thus I am rich enough how'ever poore,
I'l covet for noe wealth, wish for noe more.

On Affliction.

Feare of an after-clap makes many store
   Themselves with worldly wealth,
     Still labour more,
   And many to prevent
   Sicknes, doe purge in health   5
Phisicke ere the disease, thus God doth deale,
   By punishment
Prevents, and hinders such as wound, and steale
   His honour by offensive sinne,
And good it is they have afflicted beene.   10

Affliction is a sure, and certaine signe
   Of Gods exceedinge love,
     'Tis the divine
   Expression of his care
   By which he strives to move   15
His from their follies, and would teach them come
     With reverent feare
And hearty penitence to heaven their home.
   O bless'd affliction that do'st winne
Sinners, 'tis good they have afflicted beene.   20

If thou afflict me Lord, ô grante me grace
   I may submit to thee,
     And still imbrace
   It as thy sacred hand,
   And ever better'd be,   25
May it kill sinne in me, afflict me then
     I'l not withstand
But humbly (spight of all malignant men)
   Blesse thee, and kisse thy rod, nor lin
To praise thy name I have afflicted beene.   30

Lord I confesse thy goodnes thou hast show'd

Exceedingly to me,
   And still bestow'd
Infinite blessings on
   My fraile mortalitie.   35
But this the least, for thou in mercy hast
   Still scourg'd me from
My ill, and by affliction made me tast
   My guilt, I pray thee let it be
Happie for me, thou hast afflicted me.   40

On health.

The richest blessinge life allowes
     Mortalitie
     Is for to be
In perfect health, who wants that knowes
     Noe happinesse,   5
     Though wealth doe blesse
Exceedingly his dayes, yet without health
Noe ioy, noe comfort's to be found in wealth.

Health 'tis the poore mans God,
     The rich man's gaine,   10
     (Phisitions paine)
Of such esteeme that all goes od
     And nothinge is
     Reckon'd for blisse
Below, if that be wantinge, Monarchs sway   15
Is but a torment, if that be away.

Though health soe greate a blessinge be
     To th'body, yet
     It is noe whit
Worthy compare to th'sanitie,   20
     And health of mind,
     For man will find
How'ever seeminge sound his flesh appeares,
His mind distracted with a thousand feares.

Though sicknes presse my outward part   25
     Then, let me be
     Lord vnto thee
Sound, and vntainted at my heart,
     And as I pine
     I'th'flesh, refine   30
And strengthen thou my inward man, then I
(Although my body faile) shall never die.

On the Inscription over the

Anacrostica. Joh: 19. Cap: v: 19.

I   am that Saviour that vouchsaf'd to die
E   ven I my selfe that was content to be
S   uffer'd the death o'th'Crosse, suffer'd noe lesse
V   nto the world might come, and peace ensue
S   uffer I did such wounds, such killinge grones   5

O   let it pittie then move in you soe
F   erret remorse, and that inioyne you doffe

N   oe more let sinne abound, but may contrition
A   ll else in vayne I suffer, and Abba
Z   eale is but cold in you, how'er the blaze   10
A   ll your devotion is not worth a flea
R   epent then quickly that my sepulcher
E   ver remember him that did denye
T   he miserie of you; for my sake sett
H   imselfe with the worlds businesse, I am nigh   15

T   rust not in worldly wealth for cancker'd rust
H   eape vp your treasure, for in heaven nor moth,
E   arth, and its choycest pleasures are but drosse

K   nit, and ingrafted into me, the racke
I   will be with you still, pittie your crie   20
N   ot death it selfe shall hurt you, I vpon
G   lorie shall your reward be, every dreg

O   ff you shall purged be, and you shall know
F   eare not then quickly for my sake to doffe

T   hen shall you welcome be, for I was sent   25
H   eale such as seeke for ease, bestowe new birth
E   ven for such, and none but such I give

I   will revenge my bloud on those that flie
E   ven in the flames of hell, and may a curse
W   ell I am come to heale, and as I bowe   30
E   ternallie themselves to me, and keepe
S   orrow shall be exil'd, and I noe lesse

head of Christ on the Crosse.

Anacrostica. Joh: 19: Cap: ver: 19.

For sinsicke soules, behold me it is	I
Scourg'd, buffeted, despis'd, bethorn'd for y	E
Then all my Fathers wrath that happine	S
To those that would repent, to heaven be tr	V
As would have mov'd to ruth the senceles stone	S 5
As may constraine you to repentance g	O
Sinnes damned garment, and all vice put of	F
For me, and for your sinnes make good remissio	N
In vaine you crie havinge not learn'd your	A
May make such as your selfe with wonder ga	Z 10
Vnlesse it have more then an outward ple	A
May bury all your sinnes, and may you eve	R
Noe paines, noe torments, that might remedi	E
Light by all pleasure, and let noe man fre	T
To all that love me, will assist from hig	H 15
Will soone consume it, but amonge the ius	T
Nor thiefe, nor can consume, nor pilfer dot	H
And rob the soule of blisse, then flie such loss	E
Ye need not feare, though whips furrow your bar	K
Wipe off your teares, make your tormentours d	I 20
Your heads (in spight of death) will sett the Crow	N
Of fraile mortalitie, and pollutions rag	G
Eternall pleasures, 'stead of these bel	O
Sinnes damned garment, and all vice put of	F
Only to save such as are peniten	T 25
On the repentant, and obedient eart	H
Freely my life that they may ever liv	E
Farre from my love, for ever let them fr	I
Fall on them greater if there may be wors	E
For sinners, soe I would have them to vo	W 30
Those vowes most constant, then though now I weep	E
Happie in death, then you in happine	S

On Baptisme.

Nature affords vs flesh, and there
      Leaves vs, soe every beast
  May boast a share as large as man
Within his infant age, while yet he can
      Discerne noe more at least,   5
        But Christians are
(When once they Christians are, though ne'r soe younge)
By Baptisme number'd 'mongst the sacred thronge.

  It is that holy water makes
        (Vs'd with the pow'rfull name   10
  Of Father, Sonne, and Holy Ghost)
Our spotted soules be white, before neer lost,
      I'th'drosse, and dirt of shame,
        'Tis that which takes
Natures corruption from vs, thus anew   15
Our dead flesh quick's made by this sacred dew.

  Thus wash'd, we are incorporate,
      And members made, and knitt
  Into the Church Catholicall,
Strengthen'd 'gainst temptings diabolicall,   20
      Soe happie maketh it
        The sad soules' state.
O blessed Sacrament that doth vnite
Vs to the Church, polluted makes vs white.

  Eternall Father how shall I   25
      Thy sacred name exalt,
  Was't not enough thou madest me
Man to thy likenes, but thou still must be
      Mindfull to purge my fault,
        And purifie   30

Me from my parents sinne originall,
And both from sinne, and death me disinthrall?

    What's man, or what am I the worst
        That thou should'st thus provide
    A sacred Laver, royall-bath
To cleanse (assoone as borne) my soule which hath
        Beene bless'd, and rectifi'd
          (Though once accurss'd)
To heaven, and thee, and I am now become
By thy decree, coheire with God-the-Sonne.

Inspire me with thy goodnes that I still
May growe in virtue, and abhorre all ill.

On Balaam, and his Asse.

Whither thou sonne of Beor hasts thou soe,
Or why with these associates do'st thou goe?
      Doth it befit
A man of God with such as these to sitt,?
      Art thou become   5
A Moabite with them? or hath the summe
Of divination brought thee made thee feare
      Noe fate, nor care
    For thy greate Lord's commands?
O powerfull wealth, when such an one as this   10
Will leave his God for gold, forsake his land
And goe with strangers, forfeite his soules blisse.

Think'st thou, thou canst with safety reach the end
Of thy forbidden iourney, and attend
      On Moabs Kinge   15
Though god forbid thee, knowe that God will bringe
      Vnlook'd for ill
Vpon thy head, horrour and griefe shall fill
Thy vnderstandinge parte, thy faintinge asse
      Would bid thee passe   20
    Noe further, could shee speake;
But thou wilt on though a sword's point's i'th'way
To stop thy passage, and resolv'd wilt breake
Thorough, although an Angell bid thee stay.

The Seer is become a verier asse   25
Then is the beast he Rides on, and alas
      But for that beast,
Had ere he further pass'd, beene left to feast
      Th'impartiall wormes:
And while he kicks, and beates, and fumes, and stormes   30
'Gainst the poore Asse, the asse bespeaks him thus,

   Is this righteous
   Thrice to correct me, when
I am not faulty, am not I your asse
Which all your life y'ave rid on, wherefore then   35
(Since never vs'd to faile, forbid to passe

By th'angells threatninge hand who thwarts your way)
Spend you your rage on me? be wise, and stay.
   Nor could this strange,
Vnheard of miracle i'th'beast, once change   40
   His firme intent,
But she should die had he a sword, soe bent
He was on his owne will that on he would,
   Oh that man should
   Be soe rebellious still   45
Against his Gods commands; him selfe had put
His reason's eyes out, and deprav'd his will,
And God in iustice did his bodies shutt:

But now he sees the Angell, and in showe
Would have return'd, but is commanded goe   50
   His iourney on,
Glad of commaund he goes, although 'twere done
   Because it was
Indeed his owne desire, soe that (alas)
The precept proves his curse, himselfe shall loose   55
   Himselfe, nor choose
   But blesse, where he would curse;
And 'cause he would not virtuous live, shall die
Amonge the heathens like a beast, or worse,
Such is the end of base Cupiditie;   60

Contempt of's god, and fond desire of gaine
Hath switch'd, and spurr'd him to eternall paine.

On the three Children in the fierie fornace.

Ye glorious Ioue-borne ympes how you reioyce
Your heavenly Sire to heare your swanlike voice
Chaunt forth (in spight of death) his sacred praise,
Behold the flames dance at your pow'rfull layes
And feare to hurt you, fire for love of you   5
Shall become cold as ice, yet shall renew
Its naturall fiercenes to destroy your foes,
Angells shall guard you soe, you shall not loose
The smallest hayre, and though but three are bound
In spight o'th'tyrant-kinge there shall be found   10
A fourth, (all walkinge loose) whose glorious face
Shall fright th'insultinge monarch, and his base
Shallow-brain'd Sophi; thus both can, and will
Th'eternall worke for his owne servants still.
The water shall be parted, and shall stand   15
On each side like a wall, while on drie land
Through it the Saints shall passe, the earth shall yield
Suddenly choice delights, and every field
Through which they goe shall grone vnder the weight
Of natures choycest fruite, the fire shall streight   20
Lay off its native burninge, and shall be
Ready to serve such without iniurie,
At mid-day shall the Sunne stop his carriere
And ten degrees shall backe againe retire,
The heavens, and starres by course, shall warre and fight   25
Against all such as keepe them from their right,
And all the Elements with one consent
Shall strive to shield, and guard the innocent,
This is th'Almightie's worke, and none but he
Did in the burninge flames preserve these three.   30
And didd'st thou thus for them because in thee
Alone, they trusted? Lord instruct thou me

Also I humbly begge, that I may love,
And trust in thee alone, then though thou prove
Me by the flame, the sword, or plague I dare   35
Build on thy mercy, and despise all feare
Even in the midd'st of death; thy only name
Shall arme me 'gainst the racke, plague, sword, and flame.

On Wisedome.

W'are bruites by nature, and doe knowe
Noe more then they, a manlike shape
If without reason, doth but showe
Rude, and as beastlike as an ape,
'Tis sacred wisedome makes men growe,   5
And steeres them to the heavenly cape,
Only the wise man knowes his way,
The foolish goe but often stray.

Discretion, and experience
With naturall-knowledge are as stayres   10
By which to wisedomes eminence
We doe attaine, and all our cares
O'th'world must give preheminence
To her, and her divine affaires,
Who courts this mistresse must bringe fire   15
From the divine celestiall quire.

This heaven-borne beauty will despise
The richest clods of senceles earth,
Laugh at the amourous fooleries
Of the vsurious worldlings mirth,   20
The Roarer though he sweare his lies,
She knowes a coxcombe from his birth,
And though the Courtier fawne and flatter
She hates him for his want of matter.

The Scholler who is seeminge wise   25
And therefore high exalted is,
Within his owne conceit, she spies
His shallow pate doth learninge misse,
The Levite she would faine advise
To leave his pride, and lazines,   30
It grieves her if she chance to find

In such an avaritious mind.

The greatest Polititians gaine
From her a scornfull slight respect,
Too well shee knowes them, nor will staine   35
Her honour to soe small effect,
Their high-heel'd plots for her are vaine,
And gaine them but the more neglect,
And since *Achitophell*, she hates
Such profound, high, aspiringe pates.   40

Noe 'tis the noble humble wight
She will converse with, and be knitt
Only to him that makes delight
A stranger to him, who noe whitt
Staggers with all the ponderous weight   45
Affliction ere did lay on it,
But labours through the worlds worst ill,
To gaine the rich, celestiall hill.

There wisedome dwells, and only there
May she be found; who iourney thither   50
Her divine favour need not feare,
But shall have leave to solace with her,
Freed from affliction, griefe, and care,
Where ioyes are greene, and never wither.
In vaine's all knowledge but what tends   55
To heaven-ward, and in folly ends.

The worlds wisedome is foolishnes,
And such as brings reproach alonge,
But heavenly leads to happines,
And teaches vs to suffer wronge.   60
'Tis shallow wisedome that doth blesse
Noe longer then the party's stronge.
Lord though I foolish be belowe,
In heavenly wisedome make me growe.

On the name Christians.

Anacrostica. [I]

C hristians in name, and not in nature strange,
H is, are noe turnecoates, and this impious change
R eports you doe vsurpe his livery,
I mplies you would betray him, and would be
S ome of the Iudas-number, but take heed   5
T he best of Iudas fate, was traytour's meed;
I 'l pray for better lucke, our master to
A loud, himselfe bespeaks vs, that we doe
N othinge against his honour, I will than
S trive in my heart to be true Christian.   10

Another. [II]

C hrist's was a life of trouble, from his birth
H is Cradle, to his death, devoyd of mirth,
R eady to suffer all with patience, still
I ntreatinge pardon for his sterne foes ill,
S orrow, and griefe his constant company,   5
T ormented beyond patience, yet he
I n all things did forgive, and freely gave
A ll things to all, that heartily did crave,
N ow if you would his true disciples be
S trive to be like him in integritie.   10

Another. [III]

C an we beleeve it is enough to weare
H is coate, and cognizance, and yet forbeare
R espect, and service to him? shall we seeme
 I n name, and outside Christ's, and not within?
S hame, of all shames; are we soe impious as   5
T o damne our selves by sinne, and yet would passe
 I n at the gate of heaven as Saints of his?
A las, we foole our selves out of our blisse.
N one but who like him righteous strive to be,
S hall share with him in his eternitie.   10

Another. [IV]

C ount all as doinge for Christ whose name ye beare,
H im make the obiect of your love and feare,
R elie on him alone, and let his paine
 I nstruct you not to make his bloud in vayne,
S hunne sinne, and sinnes infection, suffer all   5
T o gaine a Christ with patience, if he call
 I n fire, famine, plague to fetch ye hence,
A lone beguard ye with his innocence,
N umber'd ye shall be then 'monge those whom he
S hall please to cloath with his owne puritie.   10

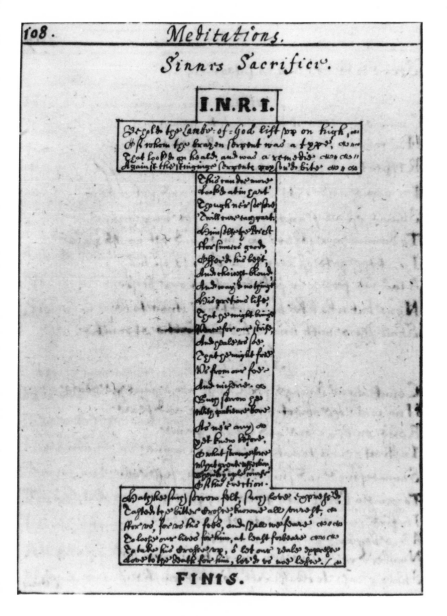

"Sinnes Sacrifice"
James Marshall and Marie-Louise Osborn Memorial Collection
Beinecke Rare Book and Manuscript Library
Yale University

Sinnes Sacrifice.
I.N.R.I.

Behold the Lambe-of-God lift vp on high,
Of whom the brazen serpent was a type,
That look'd on heal'd, and was a remedie
Against the stinginge serpents poyson'd bite.
      This can doe more,   5
      Look'd at in hart
      Though ne'r soe sore,
      'Twill cure each part.
      Himselfe the Priest
      For sinners good,   10
      Offer'd his best,
      And choicest bloud,
      And way'd no thinge
      His pretious life,
      That he might bringe   15
      Peace for our strife,
      And heale vs soe
      That he might free
      Vs from our foe
      And miserie.   20
      Such sorrow he
      With patience bore
      As ne'r any
      Yet knew before,
      O what strange force,   25
      What greate affection,
      Shew'd the whole course
      Of his erection.
Hath he such sorrow felt, such love express'd,
Tasted the bitter Crosse, knowne all vnrest   30
For vs, for vs his foes, and shall we feare

To loose our lives for him, at least forbeare
To take his Crosse vp, ô let our zeale expresse
Love to the death for him, lov'd vs noe lesse.

FINIS.

Appendix

On the fly-leaves at the end of the July manuscript is a poem written in some later hand. It does not appear in the British Museum Index for manuscript poetry, and I have been unable to identify it. The poem is unrelated to the poetry in Colman's *Divine Meditations*, but I am including it as a distinctive marking on the July manuscript.

> Of Absent Daphnis, Lycidas Complains,
> And fair Amintas answers the Strains,
> boath Sheepherd Swains, & boath in youths full Pride
> Where Yellow Tiber Rols his rapid tide,
> And tamd the river with their plaint[i]ve str[ai]ns;
> Sing O Ye Nine, the sorrows of the swains;
> Sing: for the Rocks, (if we may credit give)
> Forgot their Nature, & began to Live,
> And the pleas'd Stream its wandring Cours Delayd,
> And Idly Loytring, ore the Pebles Strayd,
> Then first Strove Lycidas his Pipe to fill,
> Amyntas yeild, to Lycidas in skill.
>
> L. Go Gentle Gales, & bear my Sighs away,
> (tis all I ask) to Lovely Daphnis say,
> Ah beauteous Swain tho absent how or [sic] Greif
> That thou shoulds know it would be some releif,
> Wheather unmindfull of thy faithful Swains,
> Widowd Flocks that grase upon the plains,

[new page]

> Thy Much Lovd Tuscan fields thy presence boast,
> Lost the sweets of fertill Latiums Coast,
> for Ancient Latum a Much honourd Name,
> & Haary Tibiers Yellow-Gliding Stream,
> You Chuse a fresher Zephir to inhale,
> & breath the Sweets of Beautious Arno-Dale.

Commentary

Commentary

Title page—May

Philo-musus: lover of the muse.

Studiosus diem diuidit, Otiosus frangit: 'The zealous student apportions the day; the idle man shatters it in pieces.' I have not been able to identify the source of this epigraph; perhaps Colman himself composed it. The opposition of *dividere* and *frangere* can be found in Cicero, *De Finibus* 2.9.26.

Letter to William Rokeby, Esq. (p. 57)

William Rokeby, Esq.: Probably Sir William Rokeby (1599–1665), of Hotham and Skiers, Yorkshire, who was created a baronet 29 January 1660/1. He was the son and heir of William Rokeby, esq. of Hotham (1556–1626) and Dorothy, daughter of William Rokeby, esq. of Skiers. He married Frances, daughter of Sir William Hickman, Knt., of Gainsborough, Lincolnshire.

4–5 *Horae succissivae*: leisure hours; it is the title of a book of prose meditations by Joseph Henshaw, D.D. (1603–79), a loyal Anglican churchman, persecuted during the Civil Wars, but rewarded afterward by a "rapid succession of dignities" and ultimately with the bishopric of Peterborough in 1663 [D.N.B.]. The first recorded edition of *Horae Succisivae, or, Spare-Houres of Meditations; Upon our Duty to God, Others, Ourselves* is S.T.C. 13167, the second edition, entered in 1630 and printed in 1631; there were five editions of *Horae Succisivae* by 1640.

15 *Primogenitus ingenij*: the first offspring of wit or talent. Cf. Donne, "The Progresse of the Soule," ll. 33–36.

19 *illustrate*: set in a good light, display to advantage.

21–23 *Non fonte . . . Memini*: First lines of the prologue to the *Satires* of Persius. "I never soused my lips in the Nag's Spring [the inspiring spring Hippocrene, struck out by the hoof of Pegasus, on the top of Mount Helicon]; never, that I can remember, did I dream on the two-topped Parnasus" (Loeb Classical Library, *Juvenal and Persius*, English translation by G. G. Ramsey, p. 310). The Loeb text reads *Nec* in line 1, where Colman writes *Non*.

26   *that salt, that seasoninge*: Cf. Leviticus 2:13.

Anacrostica Dedicatoria. [I] (p. 59)

Numbered by editor.

Title   *Anacrostica*: Colman seems to have made up this word out of logical Latin components: *an-*, a contracted form of *ambi-*, an inseparable prefix meaning "around, round about," and *acrostichis*, an acrostic, a "poem (or other composition) in which the initial letters of the lines, taken in order, spell a word, phrase, or sentence." [O.E.D.] The acrostic is an exercise in verbal dexterity that Colman frequently used. Contemporary examples may be found in Sir John Davies's *Hymns of Astraea* (1599), in which he composes three acrostics to "ELIZABETHA REGINA"; Ben Jonson's *Epigrammes* (1616), #40, "On Margaret Ratcliffe"; and a dedicatory poem by R.N. to Joshua Sylvester's *Du Bartas His Divine Weekes and Workes* (1641).

Anacrostica Dedicatoria. [II] (p. 60)

Numbered by editor.

6   *most*: "all" is canceled; "most" is interlined and written in the margin.

13   'That your after-life may be crowned, although this life be gray (or sad).'

Anacrostica Dedicatoria. [III] (p. 61)

Numbered by editor.

Title   *Anagramma*: anagram, the transposition of the letters of a word by which another is formed, preserving the same letters.

6   *this*: refers to "mind" (line 2).

Anacrostica Dedicatoria. [IV] (p. 62)

Numbered by editor.

Title page—July

Philo-poeticus: lover of poetry.

Letter to Sir William Savile, Bart. (p. 65)

Sir William Savile, Bart.: Third Baronet of Thornhill, second son of Sir George Savile of Thornhill, and Anne, sister of Sir Thomas Wentworth, the earl of Strafford. He was sent to the Short Parliament in 1640 and in 1643 was appointed governor of York. He died 24 January 1643/4. His son was George Savile, first marquis of Halifax, prominent in Restoration politics and author of *The Character of a Trimmer.*

4   *labour*: spend labour upon, till, cultivate. Cf. Herbert's "Affliction (IV)," ll. 25–28.

> Then shall those powers, which work for grief,
>> Enter thy pay,
>> And day by day
> Labour thy praise, and my relief;

9   *Primogenitus*: the firstborn.

12   *Salem Ingenij*: acuteness of wit. Latin accusative form of *sal, salis,* "salt"; figuratively, intellectual acuteness, good sense.

Anacrostica. (p. 67)

4   *W hat*: whatever.

7–10   See biographical sketch above.

16   *E xactly*: "E asily" is canceled with an underline; "E xactly" is written in the margin with an asterisk.

21   'May no sad misfortune . . .'

The Invocation. (p. 69)

Cf. "The Invocation" to Francis Quarles's *Emblemes* (1635) and "The Printers to the Reader," the preface written by Nicholas Ferrar to Herbert's *The Temple*:

> The dedication of this work having been made by the Author to the *Divine Majestie* onely, how should we now presume to interest any mortall man in the patronage of it? Much lesse think we it meet to seek the recommendation of the Muses, for that which himself was confident to have been inspired by a diviner breath then flows from *Helicon.*

The Altar. (p. 71)

This poem shows the strong influence of George Herbert's poem, "The Altar," which is similar in shape and content. It is untitled in the May manuscript.

1–4   Cf. Herbert's "The Altar" and Quarles's *Divine Fancies* (1632), I, 93, "On Offerings."
Cf. also Psalm 51:17 [Coverdale]: "The sacrifice of God is a troubled spirit: a broken and contrite heart, O God, shalt thou not despise."

On God's Mercie. (p. 72)

9–12   Cf. Jeremiah 18:2–6 and Isaiah 64:8.

19–21   Cf. Romans 2:28–29: "For he is not a Jew, which is one outwardly; neither is that circumcision, which is outward in the flesh: But he is a Jew, which is one inwardly; and circumcision is that of the heart, in the spirit, and not in the letter; whose praise is not of men, but of God." Cf. also Deuteronomy 10:16, Jeremiah 4:4, and Colossians 2:10–11.

20–21   Cf. Herbert's "H. Baptisme (II)," line 8: "Let me be soft and supple to thy will."

22   *rowle*: roll, i.e. a register.

On my enemies vniust malice. (p. 73)

Cf. Herbert's "The Quip." For possible biographical reference, see the dedicatory letter to William Rokeby, p. 57. A type of poem defined by Puttenham in *The Arte of English Poesie*, chapter 29:

A certaine auncient forme of poesie by which men did vse to reproch their enemies . . . either in deede or by word, he will seeke reuenge against them that malice him, or practise his harmes, specially such foes as oppose themselues to a mans loues. . . . And this was done by a maner of imprecation, or as we call it by cursing and banning of the parties, and wishing all euill to a light vpon them, and though it neuer the sooner happened, yet was it great easment to the boiling stomacke: They were called *Dirae*, such as *Virgill* made against *Battarus*, and *Ouide* against *Ibis*: we Christians are forbidden to vse such vncharitable fashions, and willed to referre all our reuenges to God alone.

The Scriptural basis for this poem is Psalm 38:12–15 [Coverdale]:

> They also that sought after my life laid snares for me; and they that
> went about to do me evil talked of wickedness, and imagined deceit
> all the day long. As for me, I was like a deaf man, and heard not; and
> as one that is dumb, who doth not open his mouth. I became even
> as a man that heareth not, and in whose mouth are no reproofs. For in
> thee, O LORD, have I put my trust; thou shalt answer for me, O Lord
> my God.

2   *Mine enemies encompasse me*: Cf. Psalm 17:9 [Coverdale] and 2 Samuel
      22:4–7.

7   Cf. Psalm 57:5 [Coverdale] and Jeremiah 9:8–9.

39   *But*: "Or" M.

      prosper: prosperity.

48   *Shalt*: "Wilt" M.

On Mortalitie. (p. 75)

Cf. John Donne, *Deaths Dvell, or, A Consolation to the Soule, against the
dying Life, and living Death of the Body*, 1633, pp. 8–9.

> and hee hath given them *earth* for their *grave* and Sepulture, to *returne*
> and resolve to *earth*, but not for theyr *possession*: Here we have no
> *continuing City*, nay no *cottage* that continues, nay no persons, no
> bodyes that continue. Whatsoever mooved Saint IEROME to call the
> journeyes of the *Israelites* in the *Wildernesse*, Mansions; The word (the
> word is *Nasang*) signifies but a *iourney*, but a peregrination. Even the
> *Israel of God* hath no Mansions; but journeyes, pilgrimages in this
> life. By what measure did *Iacob* measure his life to *Pharoah*; *the dayes
> of the yeares of my Pilgrimage.* [Marginal note: Gen. 47.9] ... for this
> whole *World* is but an *vniversall Church-yard*, but our *common grave*,
> and the life and motion that the greatest persons haue in it, is but as
> the shaking of buried bodyes in theyr Grave, by an *Earth-quake*. That
> which wee call life, is but *Hebdomada mortium*, a *weeke of death*, seven
> dayes, seaven periods of our life spent in dying, *a dying seaven times
> over*; and there is an end. *Our birth dyes in infancy*, and our *infancy*
> dyes in *youth*, and *youth* and the rest dye in *age*, and *age* also dyes,
> and *determines all*.... Our *youth* is *worse* then our *infancy*, and our

age worse then our *youth.* Our *youth* is *hungry and thirsty,* after those *sinnes,* which our *infancy knew not*; And our *age* is *sory* and *angry,* that it *cannot pursue* those *sinnes,* which our *youth did*; ... so many deadly calamities accompany every condition, and every period of this life, as that death it selfe would bee an ease to them that suffer them.

Cf. also Donne's "Anatomie of the World," ll. 91–94, 129–30, 135–36.

1–2   For verbal echoes, cf. Herbert's "Repentance," ll. 4–5.

4   Cf. Psalm 39:6 [Coverdale].

5   Cf. Psalm 90:5–6 [Coverdale].

9   Cf. Herbert's "Vanitie (II)," ll. 17–18 and Quarles's *Emblemes,* I, iv, 15–18 and I, vi, 23–24.

17–24   Cf. Joseph Henshaw's *Horae Succisivae,* I, 79–80:

Mee thinkes it is but *th'other* day I came into the world, and *anon* I am *leaving* it: How time runs away, and we meet with Death alway, e're wee have time to thinke our selves alive: One doth but *breake-fast* here, another *dine,* he that lives longest doth but *suppe*: We must all *goe to bed* in another World. I will so live *every day,* as if I should live *no more*: 'tis more than I know, if I shall.

25   *to lengthen out our days*: Cf. 1 Kings 3:14 and Deuteronomy 25:15.

32   Repetition of epigraph, Genesis 47:9. Cf. Quarles's *Emblemes,* V, x, 1–3.

33   *crosse*: (adj.), adverse, opposing, thwarting. Cf. Herbert's "The Sinner," line 7.

43   *coy*: distant, disdainful.

48   Cf. Donne's "The Progresse of the Soule," ll. 399–400.

but whil'st you thinke you bee
Constant, you'are hourely in inconstancie.

49   *and*: "or" *M*; "or" is canceled and "and" is interlined *J.*

Another. (p. 77)

21   *crispe*: curl in short, stiff curls.

22   *antique*: antic—absurd, grotesque, incongruous, possibly with a pun on "antique" in the sense of "in the manner of the ancients."

29   *fondlings*: foolish people.

       On Immortalitie. (p. 79)

1   Cf. Donne's "The Progresse of the Soule," ll. 339–40.

                   Up, up, my drowsie Soule, where thy new eare
                   Shall in the Angels songs no discord heare.

14   *pose*: puzzle, perplex. Cf. Herbert's "The Church-porch," ll. 223–24, and
       "The Church Militant," ll. 51–52.

       Another. (p. 81)

9–10   Judas kept the moneybag for Jesus and the disciples (John 13:29). Cf.
       Herbert's "The Sacrifice," ll. 13–16.

                   Mine own Apostle, who the bag did beare,
                   Though he had all I had, did not forbeare
                   To sell me also, and to put me there:
                               Was ever grief like mine?

       Cf. also *Saint Bernard His Meditations*, p. 52.

       Oh thou hatefull traitor! my louing Iesus made thee one of the little
       number of his Disciples: admitted thee into the blessed societie of his
       elected, and made thee Steward of his familie, *to keepe the bag*, and
       bestow the money which was giuen to him and his Disciples....

14   *my ayd*: "mine ayd" *M*.

27   *doome*: judgment, sentence.

30–32 Cf. Luke 23:6–8, 11–12, and Herbert's "The Sacrifice," ll. 73–76.

                   They binde, and leade me unto *Herod*: he
                   Sends me to *Pilate*. This makes them agree;
                   But yet their friendship is my enmitie:
                               Was ever grief like mine?

41   *Cyrene*: Cf. Luke 23:26.

44   *houle*: howl.

62–64 Cf. Luke 23:34.

67–72 Cf. Luke 23:39–43.

75–76   Cf. The Lamentations of Jeremiah 1:12.

78   *crimes*: "sinnes" M.

On the strange apparitions at Christ's death. (p. 84)

Cf. the Gospel accounts of cosmic turmoil at the Crucifixion (Matthew 27:51, Mark 15:38, Luke 23:44) and Robert Southwell's "Mary Magdalens Complaint at Christes Death," ll. 7–10:

> Seely starres must needs leaue shining,
>   When the sunne is shadowed.
> Borrowed streames refraine their running,
>   When head springs are hindered.

12   *Sunne*: "Sonne" M.

14   *equall*: fitting, proper.

On his sweate on mount Olivet. (p. 85)

Cf. Luke 22:44: "And being in an agony he prayed more earnestly: and his sweat was as it were great drops of blood falling down to the ground."

On Christ crown'd with thornes. (p. 86)

21   *ye*: "you" M.

The Summons. (p. 88)

This is the first of a series of eight poems, which comprise a dramatized meditation of self-examination, set at the final Day of Judgment; cf. Quarles's *Emblemes*, III, x. If Colman were the "kinsman" of Rokeby (as he claims in the dedicatory letter) and frequented Rokeby's home in Hoyland Nether, Skiers Hall, then the presence there of the manorial court would have familiarized him with the legal vocabulary that abounds in these poems. See A. K. Clayton's monograph, *Hoyland Nether*, published by the Hoyland Nether Urban District Council in November 1973.

1   *O yes*: "from Old French *oiez*, *oyez*, hear ye! ... often written *O yes*! ... a call by the public crier or court officer (usually thrice uttered) to command silence and attention for the reading of a proclamation." [O.E.D.]

The Arraignment. (p. 89)

6   'Innocence must be pardoned.'

The Indictment. (p. 90)

18   The seven mortal sins are presented in procession or parade, as in the *Faerie Queene*, I.iv.18–36, where Lucifera's (Pride's) coach "was drawne of six vnequall beasts,/ On which her six sage Counsellours did ryde."

23   *rout*: disorderly crowd; noisy mob. See the note on line 18 above.

24   *Commission*: Lines 11–20 catalogue sins of commission, as opposed to sins of omission catalogued in ll. 31–40.

31ff   Cf. Matthew 25:35–40.

32   *the*: omitted in *M*.

39–40   Cf. James 1:27 and Isaiah 1:17. Cf. also the "petitions" of the litany in the *Book of Common Prayer* (1638): "That it may please thee to defend and provide for the fatherlesse children and widows, and all that be desolate and oppressed."

The Regenerate sinners plea. (p. 92)

5   *score*: the account or number of his sins.

13   *roule*: Ambiguous. "Roule" was a spelling for both "rule" and "roll" in the sixteenth to seventeenth centuries. Therefore, Colman could mean either 'a merciful ruling' or 'a list on which the names of those to receive mercy are recorded.'

15   *tri'd*: undergone. Cf. Herbert's "Praise (III)," ll. 34–35.

> to show the sore
> And bloudie battell which thou once didst trie)

The vnregenerate Sinners plea. (p. 93)

The damning sin of the unregenerate sinner, evident in his pride in his own good works, is independence of God's mercy and enabling grace; contrast his offer of testimony and evidence with the humility of "the Regenerate sinners plea," especially its last stanza. Cf. Article 13 of the *Thirty-Nine Articles of the Church of England*:

> Works done before the grace of Christ, and the Inspiration of his
> Spirit, are not pleasant to God, forasmuch as they spring not of faith
> in Jesus Christ; neither do they make men meet to receive grace ...
> yea rather, for that they are not done as God hath willed and com-
> manded them to be done, we doubt not but they have the nature of
> sin.

15–16   'My actual deeds (ll. 23–26) shall be my testimony.'

18   'as they ["the Court, and Justice"—line 6] allege.'

22   *behoofe*: use, benefit, advantage.

23–26   Cf. Matthew 25:35–40.

The veredict. (p. 94)

1   *Bill*: bill of indictment.

5   *Both*: the regenerate sinner and the unregenerate sinner.

15   *graine*: dye of scarlet hue.

25   *Test*: testimony, evidence.

The Sentence. (p. 95)

2–5   Cf. Matthew 25:32–34:

> And before him shall be gathered all nations: and he shall separate
> them one from another, as a shepherd divideth his sheep from the
> goats: And he shall set the sheep on his right hand, but the goats on
> the left. Then shall the King say unto them on his right hand, Come,
> ye blessed of my Father, inherit the kingdom prepared for you from
> the foundation of the world.

5   *dexter-hand*: right hand.

An Appendixe. (p. 96)

9   *misse*: fail to see, perceive, or understand. An awkward passage, ll. 7–10
        can be paraphrased: 'Conscience is the Accuser who in this trial will not
        understand (will intentionally disregard) all excuses offered by the accused
        and who will accept no denial of the accusations.'

15   *Grand-Inquest*: grand jury.

On Prayer. (p. 97)

1–10   The title and the first line, taken together, establish the metaphor: prayers are the soul's music, and the prayer of a soul in which the several elements are agreeably ordered is harmonious music. The speaker could become absorbed in the music (prayer) that he hears, were he not so disturbed by the cacophony of his own soul's music. He is so oppressed by his "heavy load of crimes" (line 9) that the only notes of his music (that is, prayer) are "groanes, and sighes" (line 10) which lack "Concords influence" and, hence, harmony. The image of sighs and groans as the sinful soul's music to God is frequent in Herbert's poetry; cf. "Gratefulnesse" (ll. 19–24), "Sion" (ll. 21–24), "The Search" (line 22), and these lines (14–16) from "The Crosse":

> Another [ague] in my soul (the memorie
> What I would do for thee, if once my grones
>   Could be allow'd for harmonie).

6   *To rent*: to rend, separate.

8   *would*: 'would rend that sense from all the rest.'

19   *silent hearty*: unmusical but sincere.
    drawe: induce God to "graunt/ My plaint" (ll. 15–16).

19–20   Cf. Ben Jonson's "Ode. Allegorical," ll. 47–48:

> Music hath power to draw,
>   Where neither Force can bend, nor Feare can awe.

27   *give o'r*: stop, cease.

Another. (p. 98)

4   *tisicke*: phthisis, a progressive wasting disease.

13   *happie*: happen, come to pass; with the probable pun of "make happy" or "gladden."

15   *shall*: "should" *M*.

On Death. (p. 99)

1   *I may*: 'I am dismayed'; from the obsolete verb "amay," to dismay or be dismayed, with possible overtones of "amaze."

12   *flie*: a trifling circumstance, a symbol of something insignificant; cf.
        Ecclesiastes 10:1.

        Another. [I] (p. 100)

        Numbered by editor.
        The similarity between sleep and death is frequently the subject of medita-
        tions and religious poems. Cf. Henshaw's *Horae Succisivae*, I, 3:

> Sleep is but deaths elder brother, and death is but a sleepe nicknam'd;
> why should I more feare to goe to my *grave* than to my *bed*, since both
> tend to my rest: when I lye downe to sleepe, I will thinke it my last,
> and when I rise againe, account my life not continued but restor'd.

        Cf. Herbert's poems, "Death" (ll. 21–24) and "Mortification" (ll. 1–10);
        Donne's Holy Sonnet 10 (ll. 5–6); Quarles's *Divine Fancies* (I, xviii, 11–14).

6   *culler*: color.

15   *severall*: different for each respectively.

        Another. [II] (p. 101)

        Numbered by editor.
        An echo-poem, less finely made than George Herbert's "Heaven" or
        Lord Herbert of Cherbury's "Echo to a Rock" or "Echo in a Church,"
        but of the same genre; Colman's end-words rhyme but do not always
        echo.

4   *I*: aye, yes.

        On Drunckenesse. (p. 103)

4   *Gods image*: Cf. Genesis 1:27; also Herbert's "The Church-porch," line
        48: "Wine above all things doth Gods stamp deface."

5ff   The theme of man's becoming a beast through drunkenness is common:
        Cf. Henshaw's *Horae Succisivae*, II, 12–13; Herbert's "The Church-porch,"
        ll. 35–36; Quarles's *Divine Fancies*, III, 36, "On Drunkennesse."

10   'no life more important than that of drinking.'

Another. (p. 104)

7   Cf. Jeremiah 25:27: "Therefore thou shalt say unto them, Thus saith the LORD of hosts, the God of Israel; Drink ye and be drunken, and spue, and fall, and rise no more, because of the sword which I will send among you."

8   *from*: omitted in *M*.

17–20   Cf. Donne's "The Progresse of the Soule," ll. 45–48:

> Thirst for that time, O my insatiate soule,
> And serve thy thirst, with Gods safe-sealing Bowle.
> Be thirstie still, and drinke still till thou goe;
> 'Tis th'only Health, to be Hydropique so.

Cf. also John 6:54–55: "Whoso eateth my flesh, and drinketh my blood, hath eternal life; and I will raise him up at the last day. For my flesh is meat indeed, and my blood is drink indeed."

On Marriage. (p. 105)

This poem contrasts earthly marriage (in the first four stanzas) with the marriage of the soul with God (in the last three stanzas). Earthly marriage involves the union of both bodies ("clay"—line 7) and souls ("ayerie"—line 12). Death takes away "but the worst half" (line 8); then the spiritual half (the airy or ethereal part) "soares to blisse" (line 12), to divine love's mansion in the starry heaven (ll. 9–10).

12   *ayerie*: airy, ethereal, spiritual part of human love.

14   *station*: refers to "mansion" (line 9).

23–24   Cf. Matthew 19:6 and Mark 10:9: "What therefore God hath joined together, let not man put asunder." Cf. also the closing injunction of the Solemnization of Matrimony, *Book of Common Prayer*, 1638: "Those whom God hath joyned together, let no man put asunder."

25–26   Cf. opening words of the Solemnization of Matrimony, *Book of Common Prayer*, 1638: "holy Matrimony, which is an honourable estate, ... and is commended by S. Paul to be honourable among all men."

33ff   *Happie indeed*: refers to earthly marriage described in the preceding stanzas. With the word *but* the poet turns to the subject of the soul's love for God. Cf. St. Bonaventure's *The Mirrour of the Blessed Lyf of Jesu Christ*, chap. 17, "Of the miracle done at the bridale of water torned in to wyne."

> Afterward/ what the feste was al done/ oure lord Jesu cleped John by hymself and seide: Leue this womman that thou hast take to thy wyf/ and folowe me ̃. for I schal brynge the to a better and more perfiþte weddynge than this is. And anon with oute more John lafte his wyf there and folwed Jesu.

> In the forseide processe we mowe note many thinges to oure doctrine and edificacioun: firste/ in that oure lorde Jesu wolde come and be presente at the bridale and weddynge/ he scheweth vs that matrimoyne and fleschly weddynge is leueful and ordeyned of god ̃ but in that he cleped John therfro he dooth vs to vnderstonde that gostly matrimoyne is moche more worthy and perfyte.

36   *rest*: Cf. Hebrews 4:9–11: "There remaineth therefore a rest to the people of God. For he that is entered into his rest, he also hath ceased from his own works, as God did from his. Let us labour therefore to enter into that rest, lest any man fall after the same example of unbelief." Cf. Psalm 95:8–11, the text for Hebrews 4. The writer of Hebrews uses "rest" to mean the final, perfect rest in the presence of God.

39ff   The controlling image in the following lines is the marriage of the soul with Christ; cf. the Song of Solomon.

49   *thou*: God.

On Beautie. (p. 107)

4   '[that] I admire ... ' "That" is the understood complement of "soe" in line 3.

6   *rare*: 'rare thing.'

15   *chiefely*: "only" *M*.

18   *Such*: beautiful, "angel-like" (line 11).

25–27   'I will love the outward beauty, but only while virtue grows within it.'

32   *outside*: "colour" *M*.

On Anger. (p. 108)

14   *ground* : the grave of the "friend, wife, or child" (line 10).

14–16   'Or will I leave my prosperous home to spend my life in futile lament at the graveside?'

17   'If I am with sickness . . . '

18   Cf. Job 2:7: "So went Satan forth from the presence of the LORD, and smote Job with sore boils from the sole of his foot unto his crown."

19–21   'If all pleasant hours are lost, and if I alone seem born only to be crossed . . . '

25–27   Cf. Jonah 4:6–7: "And the LORD God prepared a gourd, and made it to come up over Jonah, that it might be a shadow over his head. . . . But God prepared a worm when the morning rose the next day, and it smote the gourd that it withered."

On the names Iesus, Christ, Emanuell. (p. 109)

5   Cf. Jeremiah 46:11: "Go up into Gilead, and take balm, O virgin, the daughter of Egypt: in vain shalt thou use many medicines; for thou shalt not be cured."

6   *sacred oyle* : Cf. James 5:14: "Is any sick among you? let him call for the elders of the church; and let them pray over him, anointing him with oil in the name of the Lord."

On Lazarus rais'd from death. (p. 110)

   Cf. John 11.

5   *ensignes* : his cerements, the "linnens" (line 15).

19   *coarse* : corpse.

25–26   Cf. John 11:43: "And when he thus had spoken, he cried with a loud voice, Lazarus, come forth."

29   'If it were my Redeemer who called . . . ' or the question, 'Was it my Redeemer who called?'

My last will, and Testament. (p. 112)

The method of bequest in this poem owes much to Donne's "The Will." Cf. also his "The Progresse of the Soule," ll. 102–06:

> Thinke Satans Sergeants round about thee bee,
> And thinke that but for Legacies they thrust;
> Give one thy Pride, to 'another give thy Lust:
> Give them those sinnes which they gave thee before,
> And trust th'immaculate blood to wash thy score.

9–10   Committal of the body to the grave in the Burial Office, *Book of Common Prayer*, 1638: "we therefore commit his body to the ground, earth to earth, ashes to ashes, dust to dust, . . . "

16   *heire*: inherit.

27–28 'Yet I wish that they be careful to shun the Devil's den, . . . '

39   *his*: "thy" is canceled; "his" is written next in *M*.

40   *invest*: clothe, array. Cf. Donne's "The Progresse of the Soule," ll. 113–14.

> Thinke that they shroud thee up, and think from thence
> They reinvest thee in white innocence.

cope: A large, capelike vestment worn by priests at certain ceremonies; also, cope of heaven—the overarching canopy or vault of heaven. Colman links the image of a religious vestment with the image of Heaven itself, so that we can imagine the soul, having cast off its earthly coat of clay, clothed in the bright heavens as its reward.

48   Cf. Isaiah 1:18: "though your sins be as scarlet, they shall be as white as snow; though they be red like crimson, they shall be as wool."

49–52 '. . . that the Holy Spirit receive all thoughts, words, and works that I do come into possession of before my death and then leave holy' (possible pun on "wholly").

59–60 'To the meek, who never can fail to gain the blessed kingdom, I leave humility.'

On Time. (p. 114)

1   *Most*: "How" *M*.

2　　*The vse of Sithe and Wings,*: "The nimble vse of wings," *M.*

17–20　These lines are reminiscent of Shakespeare's sonnets on the passage of time, especially Sonnet 19, lines 1, 6:

> Devouring Time, blunt thou the lions paw, . . .
> 　　. . . swift-footed Time.

21–22　The Day of Judgment, when earthly time shall cease; cf. Revelation 10:5–6: "the angel . . . lifted up his hand to heaven, And sware by him that liveth for ever and ever . . . that there should be time no longer:"

29–32　Cf. Romans 8:13: "For if ye live after the flesh, ye shall die: but if ye through the Spirit do mortify the deeds of the body, ye shall live."

On Deformitie. (p. 116)

Cf. "On Beautie," p. 107.

13　　*owes*: owns, possesses.
　　　Cf. Donne's IVVENILIA, *or certaine paradoxes and problemes*, 2d ed., 1633, pp. 38–39, [Problem] VII. "Why are the Fairest, Falsest?" "But I think the *true reason* is, that being like *gold* in many properties . . . they would be like also in this, that as *Gold* to make it selfe of use admits *allay*, so they, that they may bee *tractable, mutable,* and *currant,* have to their allay *Falshood.*"

23　　*inside's*: 'inside is.'

33–36　This poem denies the equation of beauty with virtue. 'If I be physically ugly, I will try to make my heart beautiful with grace; if my outside be white (i.e. fair), I will strive to make my heart like it.'

On Pride. (p. 118)

1　　*still*: always.

29ff　Cf. Isaiah 14:12–15:

> How art thou fallen from heaven, O Lucifer, son of the morning! how art thou cut down to the ground, which didst weaken the nations! For thou hast said in thine heart, I will ascend into heaven, I will exalt my throne above the stars of God: I will sit also upon the mount of the congregation, in the sides of the north: I will ascend above the heights of the clouds; I will be like the most High. Yet thou shalt be brought down to hell, to the sides of the pit.

Cf. also 2 Peter 2:4 and the Epistle of Jude, verse 6.

47   ' . . . who is more inclined to slavery.'

52   *aspiringe fault*: fault of aspiring above one's proper place in the universal order, as Lucifer did (line 36).

69–70   Cf. Donne's "The Progresse of the Soule," ll. 63–64, for a similar rhetorical construction.

> To be thus stupid is Alacritie;
> Men thus Lethargique have best Memory.

On Humilitie. (p. 121)

11   *doth*: "doe" *M.*

11–20   The use of commas alone for the internal punctuation of these lines lends a fluidity of meaning that is akin to confusion. The rhetorical movement of the stanza as a whole—the condemnation, made with increasing ire and brevity, of the rejection of humility by all levels of society from the palace to the citizenry—is more clear if the reader considers lines 11–12 and lines 13–14 as units of meaning. Lines 15–17 comprise two one-and-a-half-line units, and line 18 stands by itself. With lines 19–20, the poet returns to the two-line unit in order to show fully the most reprehensible rejection of humility, its rejection by the poor themselves, who seem to have so much in common with it.

13   *angells*: an old English gold coin, picturing the archangel Michael standing upon and piercing the dragon. The pun is the subject of Donne's Elegie XI, "The Bracelet," and is used by Herbert in "The Pilgrimage," ll. 16–18:

> Here I was robb'd of all my gold,
> Save one good Angell, which a friend had ti'd
> Close to my side.

20   *lightly*: to a small extent; perhaps, also, contemptuously.

       kind: alike in nature and origin; with word play on "kind" in the sense of "generous" and "considerate." *Lightly kind* could also refer to their being alike in having few possessions.

26   *rout,*: "ranke," *M.*

31   *Angell*: Humility.

38   *herbe-of-grace*: the old name for the herb "rue." In general, a herb of virtue or valuable properties.

On the life of Christ. (p. 123)

Cf. Ben Jonson's "Ode. Allegorical," prefixed to Hugh Holland's *Pancharis* (1603).

1   *Who*: Whoever.

2   *blacke swan*: a proverbial phrase for something extremely rare or non-existent. Cf. Juvenal, *Satires* 6.165: *rara avis in terris nigroque simillima cycno* ["a prodigy as rare upon the earth as a black swan!" (Loeb Classical Library, English translation by G. G. Ramsay)].

12   *part*: breast, line 10.

14   *t'alter kind*: to change its nature. Also, a pun on "the altar kind"—the food of the Eucharist: 'no natural force (wind, sun, or fleshly form) can make the swan's breast into the holy species; only his divine origin can.'

17–20   'Blessed was the day when, for the first time, this bird of eternity did see the silver water Po, or any river.'

19   *Poe*: the Po river, in northern Italy.

21–24   'The sweetest swans that ever did sing endeavor in vain to show such tunes, such harmony as this; they may hear and learn whenever his voice doth ring out.'

34   *tun'd,*: "sunge," *M*.

37   *peere*: equal.

42   *But could noe more*: 'But could do no more.'

55–56   "birds, and swans" (line 53) is the subject of "would requite" (line 54), "receive" (line 55), and "labour" (line 56).

57   *frie*: offspring.

On his Birth. A Pastorall. (p. 125)

In the Gospel accounts of the Nativity, the Wise Men are mentioned only in Matthew, and the shepherds, only in Luke. Colman dramatizes

a dialogue between the two groups, emphasizing the difference in person-
ality and attitude between the learned Wise Man and the ignorant, but
devout, shepherds.

18   *heavenly boy*: Cf. Robert Southwell's "New heaven, new warre," ll.
        47–48:

> If thou wilt foyle thy foes with ioy,
> Then flit not from the heauenly boy.

54   *mickle*: much. Dialect, used here to characterize the shepherds as rustics.

60   *Babe*: Babe's, parallel to "Saviours," both modifying "praise."

On his Birth-day. (p. 127)

Colman defends the celebration of Christmas as a holy day and holiday
("Let none dare/ To worke hereon," ll. 5–6) against the charge of Presby-
terians and many Puritans that it was a pagan festival.

9   *nought*: "none" M.

On ioy. (p. 128)

Cf. Donne's "The Progresse of the Soule," ll. 387–89.

> And what essentiall joy can'st thou expect
> Here upon earth? what permanent effect
> Of transitory causes?

4   *poore*: "bare" M.

10   'which is not joy at all.'
        For the same general attitude, cf. Herbert's "Mans medley," ll. 3–6:

> All creatures have their joy: and man hath his.
> Yet if we rightly measure,
> Mans joy and pleasure
> Rather hereafter, then in present, is.

20   *blisse*: "ioy" M.

On Mourninge. (p. 129)

4   *make appeare,*: 'make it apparent that . . .'

12   'Our cradle [i.e. being born in Original Sin] is cause for sorrow until our death.'

13–16   Cf. 1 Corinthians 13:12: "For now we see through a glass, darkly; but then face to face."

16   *knowe,*: "owe," *M.*

17   'And even the best [worthiest] men are of joy debarred . . .'

23–24   Cf. Ecclesiastes 7:3: "Sorrow is better than laughter: for by the sadness of the countenance the heart is made better."

29   'It ["Delights," line 25] flatters us to our injury.'

        adulates: flatters basely or slavishly.

        annoy: (noun) harm, injury.

34   *keep's:* keeps us. In the reading from the May manuscript, "keepes," "us" is understood from the preceding line.

37   *sackcloth:* a sign of mourning or penitence, cf. Joel 1:13.

        clothes rent: Cf. Joel 2:13: "And rend your heart, and not your garments, and turn unto the LORD your God."

37–42   Cf. Matthew 6:16–18:

        Moreover when ye fast, be not, as the hypocrites, of a sad countenance: for they disfigure their faces, that they may appear unto men to fast. Verily I say unto you, They have their reward. But thou, when thou fastest, anoint thine head, and wash thy face; That thou appear not unto men to fast, but unto thy Father which is in secret.

43–48   'As one born in sorrow, let me always prefer the mourning life, Lord; that [mourning] instructs me to regret my ill and corrects me when I err. Clothe [surround] my earth's life with sorrow, so that my afterlife may be crowned.'

43   *still*: always.

45   *Lord*: direct address, as corroborated by the May manuscript reading, "(Lord)."

47   *Clad*: Clothe (imperative).

The Invitation. (p. 131)

2 Cf. Revelation 19:7, 9: "the marriage of the Lamb is come, and his wife hath made herself ready.... And he saith unto me, Write, Blessed are they which are called unto the marriage supper of the Lamb."

14 *That*: "As" *M*.

19ff Cf. Matthew 22:11–13:

> And when the king came in to see the guests, he saw there a man which had not on a wedding garment: And he saith unto him, Friend, how camest thou in hither not having a wedding garment? And he was speechless. Then said the king to the servants, Bind him hand and foot, and take him away, and cast him into outer darkness; there shall be weeping and gnashing of teeth.

30 See above note on lines 19ff.

31 *guilty and convicted*: refers to legal image in line 27.

On the Lords Supper. (p. 132)

1 Cf. Herbert's "Faith," line 5: "Hungrie I was, and had no meat."

42 Cf. Acts 2:42: "And they continued stedfastly in the apostles' doctrine and fellowship, and in breaking of bread, and in prayers."

To the Church. (p. 134)

20 *Iehovah-Elohim*: A Jewish name for God. "Elohim" is the genitive plural of "majesty"; the phrase, therefore, means 'Jehovah of majesties,' or 'God.'

21 *Miters*: bishops.

Minor-band: the lower orders of clergy, priests and deacons.

A vowe. (p. 135)

6 Although the terminal punctuation for this line is a comma in the May manuscript and a period in the July manuscript, I have emended with a question mark, for the clause (lines 3–6) is an integral part of the question (lines 1–2), which is punctuated with a question mark in the July manuscript.

17–20   Cf. Psalm 92:1–2 [Coverdale]: "It is a good thing to give thanks unto the LORD, and to sing praises unto thy Name, O Most Highest; To tell of thy loving-kindness early in the morning, and of thy truth in the night season."

21   *reverend*: "sacred" M.

29   *'reav'd*: stole (aphetic of "bereaved").

30–31   'or whenever I see thy wounds, death, and torment presented to me in the sacrament of Holy Communion' (in which the Laudian doctrine of the Real Presence holds that Christ's body and blood are actually present).

A Dreame. (p. 137)

In its parabolic narration of the curing of a diseased heart, this poem recalls Herbert's "Love unknown" and "Peace."

5–16   Colman uses only commas for punctuation, but the syntax of the passage is clarified by the diction, especially by the use of "then" in lines 9 and 13.

19   *coule*: cowl; the garment with a hood worn by monks, taken as a sign of monastic orders.

34   *wan*: old form of "won."

36   *to trie conclusion*: to try to conclude (end) the illness.

49   *then*: "straight" is canceled; "then" is interlined in M.

50ff   Cf. Ephesians 6:13–17:

Wherefore take unto you the whole armour of God, that ye may be able to withstand in the evil day, and having done all, to stand. Stand therefore, having your loins girt about with truth, and having on the breastplate of righteousness; And your feet shod with the preparation of the gospel of peace; Above all, taking the shield of faith, wherewith ye shall be able to quench all the fiery darts of the wicked. And take the helmet of salvation, and the sword of the Spirit, which is the word of God.

65   *earnest*: a real occurrence.

On Christ's wounded side, and the soldier. (p. 139)

7   *erection*: A setting upright; hence, the placing of Jesus on the cross.

12–13   'If nature did identify the one who tormented Jesus on the cross as a man, then Heaven forbid that he keep the name of man after that deed.'

14–16   'If the tormentor was physically human, then he took his nature from a beast and intensified its bestiality.'

18–19   'The noble soldier, when his enemy has no weapons, will try to protect him from further harm.'

22   *this*: this soldier; the one who attacked the crucified Jesus.

24   This line of the otherwise regular poem has an additional foot.

29–33   Cf. John 19:34 "But one of the soldiers with a spear pierced his side, and forthwith came there out blood and water."

33   *cordiall*: a medicine, food, or beverage which invigorates the heart. Cf. Herbert's "The Sacrifice" (ll. 158–59), "Whitsunday" (ll. 17–20), and "The Knell" (ll. 13–18); also Quarles's *Emblemes* (III, iii, 43–48).

        integritie: wholeness.

39–41   A type of the *felix culpa*, the fortunate sin, which is horrible in itself but brings with it a great good. 'By your cruel act, you gave to humanity the way to redemption.'

        On Povertie. (p. 141)

4   *golden calfe*: Cf. Exodus 32.

10   *ore*: "o'r'e" *M*. Of the two readings of this word—"ore" (*J*) meaning "precious metal" and "o'r'e" (*M*) meaning "over" or "besides"—"ore" (*J*) is preferable because (1) it appears in the later manuscript; (2) it is a particular, rather than a general, term, and thus is parallel to the three nouns that precede it; and (3) in the only other instance of two spellings of this word (p. 125, line 26), it undoubtedly means "gold or precious metal." Colman probably plays on both meanings.

18   *for*: instead of.

20   I have repunctuated with a period (replacing the comma that appears in both manuscripts) in order to avoid any confusion of "*O times, ô manners*;" (line 21) with the "ieast" (line 20).

22   *spare*: give, grant.

28   *his*: refers immediately to "any one" (line 27); a further antecedent might be "Gods" (line 25)—'God's gifts which have been given to humanity.'

29–30 Cf. Luke 14:12–14 and Joseph Henshaw's *Horae Succisivae*, II, 185:

> God is therefore bountiful to us, that we might be so to others; to feast those that cannot bid us againe, and to build for those that cannot lodge us againe, is the way to that marriage-feast, and those buildings, whose Builder & Maker is *God*: he alone hath the true use of wealth that receives it onely to disburse it.

31 *mainteyne*: "or keepe" *M.*

35–38 Refers to usury and other practices of economic exploitation. Concerning usury, cf. *The True Church: Shewed to all men, that desire to be members of the same.* by Gr. [Griffith] Williams (London, 1629), p. 438:

> the Lord said, *In the sweat of thy face thou shalt eat thy bread*; but the Vsurer eateth the labour of other men, and for the vse of his money hee vseth to get Vineyards which hee planted not, houses that he builded not, and many other things that he neuer laboured for.

> This passage from Dr. Williams's book is quoted in a collection of excerpts on the subject of usury entitled *The English Usurer. Or, Usury Condemned, by The most Learned, and famous Divines of the Church of England, . . . Collected by Iohn Blaxton* (London, 1634).

36 *corne*: generic term for "grain."

40 Cf. Matthew 5:3: "Blessed are the poor in spirit: for theirs is the kingdom of heaven."

41 *I am rich enough*: "I have wealth enough," *M.*

On Affliction. (p. 143)

1 *after-clap*: a disaster or blow subsequent to some event or occurrence.

3 *Still*: always.

4–10 Cf. Joseph Henshaw's *Horae Succisivae*, I, 16–17:

> Afflictions are the medicines of the minde, if they are not toothsome, let it suffice, they are wholesome; 'tis not required in Physicke that it should please, but heale, unlesse we esteeme our pleasure above our health.

9 *offensive*: Colman uses the word to mean both "aggressive, attacking" and "displeasing, annoying, insulting."

11–15   Cf. Joseph Henshaw's *Horae Succisivae*, I, 13: "'Tis a good Signe, when
GOD chides us, that He loves us, nothing more *proves* us His than blowes,
nothing sooner *makes* us His." In *The Temple*, Herbert has written five
poems entitled "Affliction," which reflect this general attitude toward
suffering; see especially "Affliction (III)," ll. 1–4; "Affliction (IV),"
ll. 25–30; "Affliction (V)," ll. 9–10, 19–22. Cf. also 2 Corinthians 4:16–
17: "For which cause we faint not; but though our outward man perish,
yet the inward man is renewed day by day. For our light affliction, which
is but for a moment, worketh for us a far more exceeding and eternal
weight of glory."

24   *It*: affliction.

26   *it*: affliction.

29   *lin*: cease, discontinue.

40   In the May manuscript, "On Affliction" ends at the bottom of fol. 39.
The catchword to the next page, "The," is apparently erroneous, for the
next page contains the double acrostic, "I am that Saviour that vouchsaf'd
to die..." which is untitled in the May manuscript. On every other
page, the catchword duplicates the first word or syllable on the following
page, be it a part of the title or the initial word of a line of poetry. Therefore,
we may assume that this catchword refers either to a title to the double
acrostic that Colman did not transcribe to avoid overcrowding the page,
or to a poem that Colman decided not to include in this volume.

On health. (p. 145)

Not in *M*.

On the Inscription over the head of Christ on the Crosse. (pp. 146–47)

Anacrostica: See note above for page 59. Cf. John 19:19: "And Pilate
wrote a title, and put it on the cross. And the writing was, JESUS OF
NAZARETH THE KING OF THE JEWS." The title and the epigraph are omitted
in *M*.

2b   Cf. Herbert's "The Thanksgiving," line 7: "Shall I be scourged, flouted,
boxed, sold?"

5b Cf. Luke 19:39–40: "And some of the Pharisees from among the multitude said unto him, Master, rebuke thy disciples. And he answered and said unto them, I tell you that, if these should hold their peace, the stones would immediately cry out."

6b *As*: "That" *M*.

7a *that*: remorse.

8a Cf. Matthew 24:12: "And because iniquity shall abound, the love of many shall wax cold."

9a *Abba*: "Father," acknowledgement of sonship. Cf. Mark 14:36: "And he said, Abba, Father, all things are possible unto thee; take away this cup from me: nevertheless not what I will, but what thou wilt." Also, Romans 8:15: "For ye have not received the spirit of bondage again to fear; but ye have received the Spirit of adoption, whereby we cry Abba, Father." Also, Galations 4:6: "And because ye are sons, God hath sent forth the Spirit of his Son into your hearts, crying, Abba, Father."

9b *A*: aye, yes. The cry of "Abba, Father" signifies loving, filial obedience to God, in contrast to obedience through fear of reprisal. Colman is saying, "How can you possibly claim full sonship to God (by crying "Abba") when you have not yet learned the first letter of the word (and therefore, the first lesson of sonship), "A," the word of obedience?"

16–18 Omitted in *M*. Cf. Matthew 6:19–21: "Lay not up for yourselves treasures upon earth, where moth and rust doth corrupt, and where thieves break through and steal: But lay up for yourselves treasures in heaven, where neither moth nor rust doth corrupt, and where thieves do not break through nor steal: For where your treasure is, there will your heart be also." Cf. also Luke 12:33–34.

19a Cf. Romans 11:17–24, especially vv. 23–24: "And they also, if they abide not still in unbelief, shall be graffed in: for God is able to graff them in again. For if thou wert cut out of the olive tree which is wild by nature, and wert graffed contrary to nature into a good olive tree: how much more shall these, which be the natural branches, be graffed into their own olive tree?" Cf. the words of the priest after administering Holy Baptism, *Book of Common Prayer*, 1638: "Seeing now, . . . that these Children be regenerate, and grafted into the body of Christs Congregation, let us give thanks."

24   Repetition of line 7.

          On Baptisme. (p. 148)

          Not in *M*.

16   *quick's*: 'quick is.'

17–19   Cf. the Ministration of Holy Baptism, the thanksgiving, *Book of Common Prayer*, 1638: "We yeeld thee hearty thanks ... that it hath pleased thee to regenerate this infant ... with thy Holy Spirit, ... and to incorporate him into thy holy Congregation."

20   Cf. the Ministration of Holy Baptism, question for godparents, *Book of Common Prayer*, 1638: "Dost thou forsake the devill and all his works ... ?"

31   *parents*: Adam and Eve.

32   *disinthrall*: to set free from enthralment or bondage.

          On Balaam, and his Asse. (p. 150)

          Not in *M*. The story of Balaam and the ass is found in Numbers 22–24. God chose Balaam to prophesy for Him, and in spite of the riches offered by Balak which Balaam desired, Balaam, under the power of God, transmitted God's message. The role of prophet was alien to Balaam's true nature (his prophesying is an example of God's omnipotence), and as soon as he was released from the divine "spell," he "returned to his place" (Numbers 24:25). As further bits of the story appear, however, it is clear that Balaam returned, not to the Israelites, but to the Midianites. His heart being far from right and still seeking the riches that Balak had offered, Balaam helped the Moabites and Midianites seduce part of the Israelites into worshipping Baal-peor, a deity celebrated with immoral rites. Cf. Numbers 31:16: "[Moses said] Behold, these caused the children of Israel, through the counsel of Balaam, to commit trespass against the LORD in the matter of Peor, and there was a plague among the congregation of the LORD." Moses is instructed by God to avenge the death of the polluted portion of the Israelites on the Midianites, and among them is Balaam, who is slain. Cf. Numbers 31:8: "And they slew the kings of Midian, beside the rest of them that were slain; ... Balaam also the son of Beor they slew with the sword." Cf. also Joshua 13:22, 2 Peter 2:14–15, and Revelation 2:14.

13–18   'If thou thinkest that thou canst with safety reach the end of thy forbidden journey, . . . know that God will bring unlooked-for ill upon thy head.'

40   *beast,*: "asse" is canceled; "beast," is interlined with a caret.

On the three Children in the fierie fornace. (p. 152)

Not in *M*. Cf. Daniel 3 and the Song of the Three Holy Children in the Apocrypha, the Greek portion of Daniel 3, which follows verse 23.

1   *Iove-borne*: Two meanings are played on: 'carried, sustained by Jove (God)' so that the "flames dance at your pow'rful layes/ And feare to hurt you" (ll. 4–5); also, 'born of Jove (God),' as all believers are regenerate by their "heavenly Sire" (line 2).

ympes: scions (especially of a noble house); children, offspring.

3   *sacred praise*: In the Song of the Three Holy Children, the "sacred praise" is found in the songs (vv. 29–34, *Benedictus es, Domine*; vv. 35–65, *Benedicite, omnia opera Domini*) sung by Shadrach, Meshach, and Abed-nego while in the fiery furnace. These songs are used as canticles in the Order of Daily Morning Prayer, *Book of Common Prayer*.

9   Cf. Daniel 3:27: "And the princes, governors, and captains, and the king's counsellors, being gathered together, saw these men, upon whose bodies the fire had no power, nor was an hair of their head singed, neither were their coats changed, nor the smell of fire had passed on them."

13   *Sophi*: counselors.

13–14   'The Eternal will always work for his own servants.'

15ff   A list of other miracles worked in the Old Testament. Cf. John Donne's *Deaths Dvell* pp. 23–24.

> That GOD this LORD, the LORD of *life could dye*, is a strange contemplation; That the *red Sea could bee* *drie*, That the *Sun could stand still*, that an *Ouen* could be *seauen times heat* and *not burne*, That *Lions* could be *hungry & not bite*, is strange, *miraculously strange*, but *supermiraculous* that GOD *could dye*; but that GOD *would dye* is an *exaltation* of that.

15–17   Cf. Exodus 14:21–22 (Moses at the Red Sea) and Joshua 3:12–17 (Joshua's crossing the Jordan river).

17–20   Possibly, the sending of manna to feed the Israelites in the wilderness (Exodus 16:11–15), or the gift of the Promised Land, "flowing with milk and honey" (Exodus 3:8), the fruits of which they finally enjoy (Joshua 5:12).

20–22   Cf. Exodus 3:2–4:

> And the angel of the LORD appeared unto him in a flame of fire out of the midst of a bush: and he looked, and behold, the bush burned with fire, and the bush was not consumed. And Moses said, I will now turn aside, and see this great sight, why the bush is not burnt. And when the LORD saw that he turned aside to see, God called unto him out of the midst of the bush, and said, Moses, Moses. And he said, Here am I.

23–24   Cf. 2 Kings 20:9–11:

> And Isaiah said, This sign shalt thou have of the LORD, that the LORD will do the thing that he hath spoken: shall the shadow go forward ten degrees, or go back ten degrees? And Hezekiah answered, It is a light thing for the shadow to go down ten degrees: nay, but let the shadow return backward ten degrees. And Isaiah the prophet cried unto the LORD: and he brought the shadow ten degrees backward, by which it had gone down in the dial of Ahaz.

27   *Elements*: the four elements of ancient natural philosophy—water (ll. 15–17), earth (ll. 17–20), fire (ll. 20–22), and air (ll. 23–25). Colman has shown how they, in compliance with God's will ("with one consent") and against their own natures, "shield, and guard the innocent" (line 28).

34   *prove*: test, try.

On Wisedome. (p. 154)

Not in *M*. This poem draws on the complex Renaissance tradition of Wisdom (*Sapientia*), with distinctions made between knowledge (*scientia*) and wisdom (*sapientia*) in the manner of Augustine. As Frank Manley summarizes Augustine's definitions in his introduction to Donne's *Anniversaries*,

> *Scientia* is the knowledge of this world only. It is limited to what is perceived by the senses and represents the extent of man's wisdom in

a state of nature. *Sapientia* . . . is the knowledge of this world and the next, . . . a supernatural gift of God, . . . the direct intellectual comprehension of eternal things.

[p. 46]

Colman says (line 5) that "sacred wisedome" (i.e. *sapientia*) leads one to heaven; "naturall-knowledge" (*scientia*), though it set one on the way to "wisedomes eminence" (ll. 10–11), is in itself but foolishness and vanity (ll. 55–56). Wisedome's "divine affaires" (line 14) are preeminent over mere worldly cares, just as she is superior to the worldly powers with which people persuade themselves of their own importance. She dwells on a "celestiall Hill" (line 48) with God "where ioyes are greene, and never wither" (line 54), beyond the ills and the transitory nature of the fallen world.

Title   *Wisedome*: Sapience; also, as one of the manifestations of the divine nature of Jesus, used as the title of the second person of the Trinity—"the Wisdom of the Father."

6   *heavenly cape*: a destination: either a cape to which a boat might be steered, or, since etymologically related to "cope," "the cope of heaven"—the overarching canopy of heaven.

29   Levite: the tribe of Levi had sole responsibility for priestly acts in Israel; hence, a disparaging term for a clergyman or a domestic chaplain.

39   *Achitophell*: David's counselor, who gave his allegiance to David's son Absalom when it seemed that Absalom was stronger in the people's affections than his father; the type of the power-hungry, egotistical, self-seeking politician. Cf. 2 Samuel 16, 17.

48   *celestiall hill*: the dwelling place of God. Cf. Psalm 3:4 and Psalm 15:1.

57   Cf. 1 Corinthians 1:18–20, 25, 27:

the preaching of the cross is to them that perish foolishness; but unto us which are saved it is the power of God. For it is written, I will destroy the wisdom of the wise, and will bring to nothing the understanding of the prudent . . . hath not God made foolish the wisdom of the world? . . . the foolishness of God is wiser than men . . . God hath chosen the foolish things of the world to confound the wise.

59   *heavenly*: heavenly wisdom.

On the name Christians. Anacrostica [I] (p. 156)

Not in *M*; numbered by editor.

1–5 'Those who claim the name Christians and whose nature [intrinsic qualities] is not strange to [different from] this name, who are truly Christ's, [these] are not turncoats [apostates]. This change to impiety in your actions shows that you wear His livery [Christ's name] fraudulently and implies that you, like Judas, would betray him.'

7–9 'I'll pray aloud to our Master for better luck (than "traytour's meed," line 6); Christ himself exhorts us to do nothing against his honor.'

9 *than*: then, therefore.

Another. [II] (p. 156)

Not in *M*; numbered by editor.

Another. [III] (p. 157)

Not in *M*; numbered by editor.

2 *His coate*: refers to the image "livery" in "On the name Christians. Anacrostica [I]," line 3.

cognizance: In heraldry, a crest or badge to identify the retainers of a noble house; here, a reference to the speaker's claim to bear the name of Christian.

Another. [IV] (p. 157)

Not in *M*; numbered by editor.

Sinnes Sacrifice. (p. 159)

The illustration shows how Colman defines this poem as a cross by drawing the shape and then by filling out short lines with ornament. The shape of the poem reflects its content, a meditation on the Crucifixion; the inscription I.N.R.I. ("Iesus Nazarenus, Rex Iudaeorum") was placed over Christ's head by Pilate and serves to link this poem with the previous poem in the May manuscript, "On the Inscription over the head of Christ on the Crosse" (p. 146). The title is omitted in the May manuscript.

1   *Lambe-of-God* : Jesus, as the sacrifice erected on the cross for the sins of humanity; the New Testament type of the Passover Lamb (Exodus 12:3). Cf. John 1:29: "The next day John seeth Jesus coming unto him, and saith, Behold the Lamb of God, which taketh away the sin of the world." Also, *Agnus Dei*—"O Lamb of God, that takest away the sins of the world, have mercy upon us"—a hymn sung during the Eucharist. As J. H. Strawley writes in *Liturgy and Worship*, "the *Agnus Dei* was introduced as a form of Eucharistic devotion, to be sung while the Fraction was proceeding" (p. 354). The Fraction is the breaking of the Host (or Communion wafer) that represents the Body of Christ; the Host is elevated at the time of the Fraction. Thus, line 1 refers both to the Crucifixion itself and to its "reenactment" in the Eucharist.

        lift: old form of the past participle of the verb "to lift."

1–4   Of the brass serpent that Moses made, cf. Numbers 21:5–9, and John 3:14–15.

13   *way'd no thinge*: weighted (esteemed) as nothing.

29–34 These lines, which Colman punctuates only with commas, are composed of two rhetorical questions and a hortative exclamation. In the lines "Hath he . . . his foes," Colman expects assent to the content of the poem to this point; in lines 31–33, he expects a negative response to the question 'Shall we then fear to lose our lives for Christ and shall we shun even the initial step of taking up his cross?' On the basis of these answers, Colman joins with the agreeing reader to vow 'love even to death for Christ who has loved them to no lesser extent.'

35   *FINIS.*: omitted in *M*.

Bibliography

Ainslie, Gilbert. *An Historical Account of the Oaths and Subscriptions Required in the University of Cambridge on Matriculation, and of all Persons who Proceed to the Degree of Master of Arts.* Cambridge, 1833.

Alabaster, William. *The Sonnets of William Alabaster.* Edited by G. M. Story and Helen Gardner. London: Oxford University Press, 1959.

Bernard of Clairvaux, St. *Saint Bernard His Meditations: or Sighes, Sobbes, and Teares, upon our Saviours Passion. . . . Also His Motives to Mortification, with other Meditations.* Translated by "W. P." 4th ed. London, 1631–32.

Bonaventure, St. *The Mind's Road to God.* Translated by George Boas. New York: Liberal Arts Press, 1953.

———. *The Mirrour of the Blessed Lyf of Jesu Christ, a Translation of the Latin Work entitled Meditationes Vitae Christi, Attributed to Cardinal Bonaventura, Made before the year 1410 by Nicholas Love.* Edited by Lawrence F. Powell. Oxford: Clarendon Press, 1908.

The Book of Common Prayer and Administration of the Sacraments: And other Rites and Ceremonies of the Church of England. London, 1638.

Burke, John, and Burke, J. B. *A Genealogical and Heraldic History of the Extinct and Dormant Baronetcies of England, Ireland, and Scotland.* 2d ed. London, 1844.

Carew, Thomas. *The Poems of Thomas Carew with his Masque "Coelum Britannicum."* Edited by Rhodes Dunlap. Oxford: Clarendon Press, 1949.

Carroll, Roy. *The Parliamentary Representation of Yorkshire, 1625–1660.* Ann Arbor, Mich.: University Microfilms, 1965.

Clayton, A. K. *Hoyland Nether.* Hoyland Nether Urban District Council, 1973.

Curtis, Mark H. *Oxford and Cambridge in Transition 1558–1642.* Oxford: Clarendon Press, 1959.

Daniel, Samuel. *Tethys Festival: Or The Queenes Wake.* London, 1610.

Dix, Gregory, Dom. *The Shape of the Liturgy.* London: Dacre Press, 1964.

Donne, John. *Deaths Dvell, or, A Consolation to the Soule, against the dying Life, and living Death of the Body.* London, 1633.

———. *IVVENILIA, or certaine paradoxes and problems.* 2d ed. London, 1633.

———. *John Donne: The Divine Poems.* Edited by Helen Gardner. Oxford: Clarendon Press, 1952.

———. *The Poems of John Donne.* Edited by Herbert J. C. Grierson. 2 vols. Oxford: Clarendon Press, 1912.

The English Usurer, Or, Usury Condemned. Collected by Iohn Blaxton. London, 1634.

Fane, Mildmay. *Otia Sacra.* London, 1648.

Foster, Joseph. *Pedigrees of the County Families of Yorkshire.* 3 vols. London, 1874.

Foxcroft, H. C. *The Life and Letters of Sir George Savile, Bart., First Marquis of Halifax.* 2 vols. London, 1898.

François de Sales, St. *An Introduction to a Deuoute Life.* Translated by I[ohn] Y[akesley]. 3d ed. Rouen, 1614.

Freeman, Rosemary. *English Emblem Books.* London: Chatto and Windus, 1948.

Gardiner, Samuel Rawson. *History of England from the Accession of James I to the Outbreak of the Civil War, 1603–1642.* 10 vols. London, 1884.

Gilson, Étienne. *The Mystical Theology of Saint Bernard.* Translated by A. H. C. Downes. New York: Sheed and Ward, 1940.

———. *The Philosophy of St. Bonaventure.* Translated by Illtyd Trethowan and F. J. Sheed. New York: Sheed and Ward, 1938.

Haight, Gordon S. "The Sources of Quarles's *Emblemes.*" *The Library* 16 (1935–36): 188–209.

Henshaw, Joseph. *Horae Succisivae, Or, Spare-Houres of Meditations; Upon Our Duty To God, Others, Ourselves.* 3d ed. London, 1632.

Herbert, George. *The Works of George Herbert.* Edited by F. E. Hutchinson. 2d ed. Oxford: Clarendon Press, 1964.

Heywood, James, and Wright, Thomas. *Cambridge University Transactions During the Puritan Controversies of the 16th and 17th Centuries.* 2 vols. London, 1854.

Jonson, Ben. *Ben Jonson.* Edited by C. H. Herford, Percy and Evelyn Simpson. 11 vols. Oxford: Clarendon Press, 1925–52.

Juvenal and Persius [Loeb Classical Library]. Edited and translated by G. G. Ramsay. Rev. ed. London: William Heinemann, 1965.

Liturgy and Worship: A Companion to the Prayer Books of the Anglican Communion. Edited by W. K. Lowther Clarke, New York: The Macmillan Company, 1932.

Macray, W. D. *Annals of the Bodleian Library.* 2d ed. Oxford, 1890.

Manley, Frank. *John Donne: The Anniversaries.* Baltimore: Johns Hopkins Press, 1963.

Mann, Cameron. *A Concordance to the English Poems of George Herbert.* New York: Houghton Mifflin Company, 1927.

Martz, Louis L. *The Poetry of Meditation.* New Haven: Yale University Press, 1954.

Nuttall, Barbara. *A History of Thornhill.* Ossett, Eng.: Shaw Peace Limited, 1970.

Portraits of Yorkshire Worthies. Edited by Edward Hailstone. 2 vols. London, 1869.

Puttenham, Richard. *The Arte of English Poesie.* London, 1589.

Quarles, Francis. *Divine Francies.* London, 1632.

————. *Emblemes.* London, 1635.

Radcliffe, George, Sir. *The Earl of Strafforde's Letters and Dispatches, with an Essay towards his Life.* Edited by William Knowler. 2 vols. Dublin, 1740.

Savile of Rufford Manuscripts (Savile of Thornhill). Nottinghamshire County Record Office.

Southwell, Robert. *Saint Peters Complaint, Newly augmented With other Poems.* London, [1607–09?].

Sylvester, Joshua. *DuBartas His Diuine Weekes and Workes.* London, 1641.

Venn, John, and Venn, J. A. *Alumni Cantabrigiensis.* 10 vols. Cambridge: The University Press, 1922–54.

Webbe, George, et al. *A GARDEN of Spirituall Flowers.* London. 1630.

Whitaker, T. D. *Loidis and Elmete; or, an Attempt to Illustrate the Districts Described by Those Words by Bede.* Leeds, 1816.

White, Helen C. *English Devotional Literature [Prose], 1600–1640.* University of Wisconsin Studies in Language and Literature, no. 29. Madison, 1931.

Williams, Gr[iffith]. *The True Church: Shewed to all men, that desire to be members of the same.* London, 1629.

Index of First Lines

Index of Titles